G000162273

you&**your**

BMW

3-Series

you & your
BMW
3-Series

Richard Dredge   *Buying, enjoying, maintaining, modifying*

© Richard Dredge 2004

All rights reserved. No part of this publication may be reproduced, stored in a retrieval system or transmitted, in any form or by any means, electronic, mechanical, photocopying, recording or otherwise, without prior permission in writing from the publisher.

First published in 2004

A catalogue record for this book is available from the British Library

ISBN 1 85960 976 7

Library of Congress catalog card no. 2003113461

Published by Haynes Publishing, Sparkford, Yeovil, Somerset, BA22 7JJ, UK

Tel: 01963 442030 Fax: 01963 440001
Int. tel: +44 1963 442030 Int. fax: +44 1963 440001
E-mail: sales@haynes.co.uk
Web site: www.haynes.co.uk

Haynes North America, Inc.,
861 Lawrence Drive, Newbury Park,
California 91320, USA

Printed and bound in England by
J. H. Haynes & Co. Ltd, Sparkford

Jurisdictions which have strict emission control laws may consider any modifications to a vehicle to be an infringement of those laws. You are advised to check with the appropriate body or authority whether your proposed modification complies fully with the law. The author and publishers accept no liability in this regard.

While every effort is taken to ensure the accuracy of the information given in this book, no liability can be accepted by the author or publishers for any loss, damage or injury caused by errors in, or omissions from the information given.

Contents

3-Series ancestry and evolution. The '02 series (top centre) led to the
E21 (centre), followed by the E30 (bottom), E36 (top right) and
E46 (top left). (BMW)

Introduction

There is a very simple basic law in trading which says the value of any commodity will be dictated by the balance between supply and demand. The more demand there is for something, as long as supply can't quite match it, the values will remain high. But somehow, the BMW 3-Series manages to buck this trend, and it is for one reason – image. BMW's marketing gurus have somehow managed to put BMW into the position that every other car maker wants to be in – that of being able to constantly ramp up production yet continue to charge premium prices because everybody still wants them. Millions of examples of the 3-Series have been produced and if it wasn't for this model, BMW probably wouldn't be here today.

The huge success of BMW's compact executive is held up as one of the great marketing and manufacturing case studies of all time. While there are those who actively shun the notion of driving a 3-Series because 'everyone drives one nowadays', there can be no denying that in the compact executive sector, BMW's rivals have a very hard time trying to compete. In 2002, the BMW Group broke all records to sell more than one million cars for the first time. Within the UK it sold more cars than ever – a tally of 85,567 was the most cars it had ever shifted in that market. But the incredible thing was that despite the 5-Series, 7-Series, X5, Mini and Z3 all being in the BMW line up, over 60,000 of the cars BMW sold in Britain in 2002 were examples of the 3-Series. That's how crucial the car is to the company, and with four generations produced so far, there's no sign of its popularity waning.

When the fourth-generation 3-Series was launched in 1998, the MD of BMW Great Britain made a very odd comparison, but one that withstands scrutiny. He stated that a modern tennis racquet is clearly related to its ancestor of 50 years ago, although it has undergone tremendous change and that the same is true of the 3-Series – it is familiar, yet all-new. Obtuse yes, but by standing an E46 (fourth-generation) 3-Series next to its E21 (first-generation) predecessor, the likeness is immediately apparent.

As this book goes to press, the first artists' impressions of the fifth-generation 3-Series are starting to appear. While they may be more daring than has been seen before – thanks to the very creative input of BMW design chief Chris Bangle – there are several things that can be taken for granted before the car officially sees the light of day. One is that it will be a fantastic car to drive. Another is that it will be superbly engineered with top-notch engines and transmissions along with peerless build quality. And a third is that once more, BMW will shift every one it can build, thus ensuring the company continues to be one of the most profitable car makers around.

Acknowledgements

Many thanks to Gina Barnes in the BMW GB press office for all her help with sourcing press releases and pictures, as well as to the various tuning company representatives. These include Ahmet Erguen at MK Motorsport, Bianca Fiegl and Manuel Gebhart at MS Design, Savas Simsek at Hamann Motorsport and both Nick Godfrey and Kelly Villiers at Alpina's UK distributor, Sytners. Phil Clarke at Birds (the UK distributors for Hartge) and Nicole Spangenberg at Breyton were also very helpful. Thanks also to Kieth Townsend of Ultimate Cars. My thanks are also due to Ray Jones of Nottingham-based HAC Services for his help with what to look for when buying a 3-Series.

Evolution of BMW's compact executive

With more than three decades of compact executive car production under its belt, you need a good memory to recall a time when BMW did not produce a small luxury car. Indeed, BMW's 3-Series is now the car of choice for many aspiring young executives thanks to the company honing its image with constant references to outstanding dynamics, peerless build quality and understated elegant styling. But less than half a century ago BMW was on the brink, in danger of being swallowed whole by Daimler-Benz. Although the company survived to become one of the most profitable and successful independent marques, BMW could so easily have become a footnote in automotive history.

Having started aero engine production in 1916, BMW diversified into road transport with the introduction of the R32 494cc flat-twin motorcycle in 1923. That set the tone for the company, as it featured shaft drive and was both innovative and high quality in its production.

The first BMW passenger car was the Dixi – an Austin Seven built under licence. (BMW)

But car production did not begin until 1928, and when it did, it was by buying up the Dixi Werke of Eisenach. This tiny company had been building the Austin Seven under licence, and from 1929 the cars were badged as BMWs.

By 1932, BMW had decided to terminate its agreement with Austin and produce its own car, designed and developed in-house.

This was the 3/20PS Typ AM (for *Auto Munchen*) and although it was larger than the Seven, it was still a small car. A 782cc four-cylinder engine powered the car which was slightly bigger than the Seven's and the following year the Typ 303 went on sale, complete with a 1,173cc, six-cylinder engine.

Throughout the 1930s, BMW continued to develop its range of cars, with models such as the 309, 315 and 326 – the latter model being BMW's first four-door saloon. Powered by a 1,971cc 50bhp engine, the 326 was endowed with strong performance and alongside the four-door saloon there were two- and four-door cabriolets also available. Even at this early stage, BMW knew the value of offering variety.

The 326 stayed in production until 1941, but in the meantime the 328 had been introduced in 1936. This was the car with which BMW was competing so successfully in international motorsport before the Second World War, and although its engine was based

DID YOU KNOW?

BMW's logo is a reference to its production of aero engines, the alternately coloured quadrants in a circle representing a revolving propeller. The logo was first registered on 5 October 1917, the company name having been established as Bayerische Motoren Werke (Bavarian Motor Works), on 20 July 1917.

on the 326's, a new cylinder head provided the car with a much more impressive turn of speed. Hemispherical combustion chambers and cross pushrods raised power from 50bhp to 80bhp and as a result the car's top speed with standard trim was nearly 100mph (161kmh). In modified form, the 328 was capable of almost 120mph (193kmh)– impressive for a 2-litre car in the 1930s – and it is no surprise that although it was not especially expensive when new, the surviving examples are now highly sought after.

Post-war wreckage

Although BMW wasn't an especially large company before the war, it had at least been successful. But in the post-war period the company faced a bleak future. Not only was its Munich factory ruined by concerted bombing efforts, but its factory in Eisenach was now inside Eastern Germany. Until the situation could be sorted out, car production continued with small numbers of 327s rolling off the production lines between 1948 and 1956 while the 321 saloon had been built between 1945 and 1950. Because BMW had no factory of its own to build these cars, it was up to Baur of Stuttgart to produce them under contract – BMW's own factory wouldn't be ready until 1956. Munich motorcycle production resumed in 1948, but it was not until 1952 that cars were built there again. That first post-war car was the 501, which had been shown initially in 1951 and although it was an attractive vehicle, its styling was dated. Although the flowing bodywork is now regarded as classical, unfortunately when new it was also viewed in much the same way – and buyers did not want cars which appeared as though they were merely pre-war models that had been updated. The overall look of the 501 earned it the nickname of *Barockengeln*, or Baroque Angel – a reference to its bulbous and flowing lines which reminded people of the carved wooden figures depicted in south German and Austrian churches of the Baroque period (17th and 18th centuries).

The 501 was at first fitted with a six-cylinder, 1,971cc engine, but this was supplemented by a 2,580cc V8 in 1954 with a consequent gain in power from 72bhp to 95bhp. By 1955 a 3,168cc V8 powerplant had joined the range, to take the 501 even further upmarket, and with up to 140bhp on tap, the car became the true grand tourer it should have been from the outset. Sales continued to be slow so BMW tried a trick which would prove to be very successful several decades later – it introduced a range of bodystyles including a coupé and

The pre-war 328 is one of the most desirable BMWs ever made, thanks to its sporting success. (BMW)

a cabriolet. But whereas the strategy would prove successful much later on, it did little to improve sales in the 1950s. By 1955, the 502 had been launched, increasing equipment levels over the 501 in the process. The 2.6-litre and 3.2-litre V8s remained but the 2.0-litre engine was enlarged to become a 2.1-litre unit. For those who could not afford the 502, the 501 remained in production in 2.0-litre, six-cylinder form only. Still the company failed to make much headway despite the fact that by 1961 it was making Germany's fastest saloon – the 3200L. With a 160bhp V8 engine, this car, which was also one of the world's fastest saloons, had its roots in the 501. As that car was nearly a decade old, it was no wonder it was often overlooked by potential buyers. By the time the last of the Baroque Angels was built in 1964 – a decade after the introduction of the range – just 21,807 examples had been built.

BMW's first post-war car was the expensive V8-engined 501, made in small numbers and seen as old-fashioned even when new. (BMW)

Now extremely rare and highly sought after, the 507 marked a diversion for BMW, from the usual stuffy saloons. (BMW)

While BMW was struggling to make headway with its 501 and 502, the most sought after of all the classic BMWs had first been shown at the 1955 Frankfurt Motor Show: the 507. It was in 1954 that Ernst Loof had built a prototype sports car on the 502 chassis, with a 2.6-litre V8 engine. The project had come about because BMW's American importer, Max Hoffman, had told the factory that if BMW was to build a sports car that was capable of taking on the legendary Mercedes 300SL, he would be able to sell every example he could lay his hands on. Hoffman put forward a proposal by Albrecht Goertz as an alternative to the Loof solution and it was this car which was to go into limited production in 1956. A roadster bodystyle was chosen and there was an optional hard top for added practicality, but between the start of production in 1956 and the end in 1959, just 254 507s were delivered. The V8 engine had grown to 3.2 litres by the time the car had been put into production, and with this the 507 was able to top 120mph (193kmh). BMW claimed it was able to do 136mph (219kmh) but nobody ever managed to squeeze that much out of it – with just 150bhp available, or 165bhp for US-bound cars it is unlikely much more than 120mph would ever have been attainable. Regardless of the car's potential, it is one of the few truly valuable classic BMWs of the 20th century, partly thanks to its rarity and partly due to its beautiful styling. It was such a tragedy that BMW couldn't get its act together when trying to put the 507 into production – by the time all the problems had been sorted out, Mercedes had stolen a lead by introducing a roadster version of the 300SL. Not only was that car available with disc brakes all round but the BMW did not even have disc brakes at the front until the very end of production.

Such flights of fancy as the 507 were never going to turn BMW into the major player it wanted to be. So in a bid to increase sales substantially, in 1955 BMW moved into microcar production when it began production of the Isetta bubblecar under licence. The basic design was licensed from ISO but BMW fitted its own 245cc

Isetta marked a far bigger diversion for BMW, as the company embraced the microcar market to boost profits, albeit unsuccessfully. (BMW)

single-cylinder R45 motorcycle engine and altered the styling a little bit so it was slightly less like the original car. Sales were strong and by 1962 no fewer than 161,360 examples had been sold. A 587cc flat-twin version called the 600 was offered from 1957, and remained in production until 1959. It had stronger performance with exceptional frugality and in total, 35,000 or so 600s rolled off the production lines. But by 1959 BMW was in big trouble.

With mounting debts and little prospect of things improving, it looked as though the company was about to be swallowed whole by Daimler-Benz. BMW had relied too heavily on the production of large luxury cars such as the V8-engined 501, and not only were production costs very high and profit margins relatively low, but few people could afford to buy them. Although the Isetta had sold well, profit margins on these cars were so low that BMW wasn't earning enough capital to invest in the development of the new cars it so desperately needed. The answer was a loan for DM30 million from truck maker MAN and the result of the development work was a car called the 700. This was a small saloon powered by a rear-mounted flat-twin 697cc engine and with twin carburettors and 40bhp it could achieve over 80mph (129kmh), although it was still intended to be just an interim model. It pioneered monocoque construction for BMW and it also used semi-trailing arm rear suspension – something which had been introduced in the 600 and which BMW has stuck with ever since.

BMW's first small saloon car was the 700, but it was still seen as an economy car. Something bigger, but still affordable was needed. (BMW)

The *Neue Klasse* appears

However, what was really needed was a full-sized saloon, and in 1961 the 1500 was introduced – the first of a range of *Neue Klasse* cars that bridged the gap between the 700 and the 502. The 1500 featured the M115 powerplant (which retrospectively became one of

The 1500 saloon of 1961 introduced the world to the *Neue Klasse* from BMW. Mid-sized and affordable, it marked the start of a new beginning for the company. (BMW)

Above: The precursor to the 3-Series was the '02 series – at first the 1602, which then became the seminal 2002. (BMW)

Below: In cabriolet form the 2002 became something truly desirable, rather than merely practical and reliable. (BMW)

DID YOU KNOW?

The basic design of the M10 family of engines that saved BMW in 1961 survived until 1987. It started out with just 80bhp and powered everything from the company's small saloons of the 1960s through to Formula 1 racers in the 1980s – by which time it was producing an astonishing 1,400bhp.

The secret of BMW's success in making its cars so great to drive was the construction of its own proving ground, to test the cars to the limit. (BMW)

the members of the M10 family of engines), with a capacity of 1,499cc and a quartet of cylinders. With twin chain-driven overhead camshafts, this unit powered cars for the next 26 years with capacities ranging from the initial 1,499cc through to a 1,990cc version. Along the way were 1,573cc, 1,766cc and 1,773cc versions and when installed in the 2002 Turbo there was even a KKK turbocharger fitted to boost power to a heady 170bhp. The 1500 was significant not only because it marked a fresh start for BMW which would pave the way for a new breed of sporting saloons, but because it was the first BMW to feature the 'hockey stick' C-pillar which has been a feature of just about every production BMW ever since. This styling trait was introduced by Wilhelm Hofmeister and consequently it has become known as the Hofmeister kink.

The true precursor to the 3-Series was the 1600-2 (which became the 1602), and which was first shown at the 1966 Geneva Motor Show. It was fitted with a

1,573cc version of the M115 engine. By the time BMW's American importer Max Hoffman had been inspired to install a larger engine under the bonnet the company's future direction was set. Hoffman had suggested putting a larger engine into the car to produce something nimble that had plenty of power, but was still completely usable in everyday driving. With 100bhp on tap in place

The start of a whole new beginning – BMW could never have foreseen what the launch of the 3-Series in 1975 would lead to. (BMW)

of the 1602's 85bhp, and a much greater torque spread, the 2002 was much nicer to drive and was available between 1968 and 1976. BMW's trademark has always been to offer ever greater amounts of power to make the most of its cars' capable chassis, and so it was with the 1602 and 2002. A 105bhp version of the 1600, with Ti badging, was sold from 1967 and there was also a Ti derivative of the 2002 on offer, with 120bhp. But if that wasn't enough power there was also a 130bhp option, which generated the extra power thanks to Kugelfischer fuel injection. For just two years (1973/74) the 2002 Turbo was sold, complete with 170bhp but reliability wasn't up to the usual BMW standard, and it had ridiculous amounts of turbo lag while fuel consumption was also very high. It offered 130mph (209kmh) performance and great dynamics, which is why BMW managed to sell all of 1,672 examples within the two years of production – a period which unfortunately coincided with the fuel crisis.

It was not just engine choice which allowed BMW to maximise the sales of its cars – a range of bodystyles also ensured as many buyers as possible opted to take

This 320i was the third in a series of art cars created by BMW. Based on a first-generation (E21) car in 1977, the paint scheme was created by Roy Lichtenstein. (BMW)

the BMW route. Alongside the saloon versions of its 1602 and 2002, BMW offered convertibles (built by Baur) and Touring three-door estates. By taking this strategy the company managed to increase production from under 10,000 units annually in the early 1960s to more than 74,000 by 1966 and 221,298 in 1975. This growth that had been seen by the mid-1970s was helped along by the introduction of a six-cylinder engine to power a new range of 2.5-litre, 2.8-litre, 3.0-litre and 3.2-litre coupés and saloons. And while these cars may have been expensive, they were very highly regarded thanks to their superb build quality, well-developed chassis and excellent reliability – all still the most prominent facets of BMW cars today.

The first 3-Series

In 1972, BMW launched the 5-Series, marking a new era in the company's model development. On 2 May 1975 the first 3-Series was built, codenamed the E21, and this was followed up by the 6-Series and 7-Series released in 1976 and 1977 respectively. Although the E21, which was designed by Paul Bracq, was a clean-sheet design, it wasn't introduced to take BMW into new pastures as it was a direct replacement for the '02 series. That meant it was a small, high-quality sporting saloon which didn't feature one of the most criticised aspects of its

Above: In 1989, a second-generation (E30) art car was created, this time by Ken Done. The range-topping M3 was chosen. (BMW)

Below: For those who preferred a more sober paint scheme, the E30 road car was available in more discreet colours. (LAT)

predecessor – incredibly poor ventilation. The '02 had also been criticised for not having enough interior space and although the 3-Series was consequently 89mm longer, 20mm wider and featured a wheelbase with an extra 63mm, this growth was nowhere near enough because the new car would still be dogged by complaints about its cramped cabin. At the same time, the new monocoque was 18 per cent stiffer than the outgoing car's – something which would make a big difference to its handling. Safety had become one of the big issues of the early 1970s, so when the E21 was being developed it was only natural that crumple zones were incorporated into its structure and the passenger cell was much stronger than the '02's. Ergonomics were also starting to become much more considered, and the E21 set a standard which has been pursued ever since by BMW. Whereas most manufacturers were constructing a dashboard which was flat and featured scattered switchgear, the new 3-Series had a facia which was angled towards the driver and which was thoughtfully laid out with regard to both the types of controls and their layout – from here on the 3-Series would be the benchmark for dash design.

Under the skin, BMW had focused on providing a sporting drive, but it did not need to start again as the '02's suspension provided the right basic formula. There were MacPherson struts at the front, but instead of the A-arms of the '02, there were lateral links, with the anti-roll bar acting as a bottom wishbone to locate the wheels longitudinally. The front springs were 25 per cent softer to improve ride comfort but to compensate for this the anti-roll bar was stiffened up so that the car didn't wallow too much on corners. A coil-sprung semi-trailing arm system was used at the back, which was 40 per cent stiffer to help reduce pitching, but although this set-up made the E21 a sporting drive, it also led to unpredictable handling when cornering enthusiastically in the wet. ZF rack-and-pinion steering replaced the worm-and-roller system of the '02 and there were larger brakes all round – ventilated discs at the front being standard on all cars.

None of the cars was powerful – the 316 could muster just 90bhp while the range-topping 320i could manage 125bhp. As a result the cars weren't especially fast, with top speeds ranging between 99mph and 112mph (159–180kmh) – in 2003, even the entry-level 316Ti Compact could top 125mph (200kmh). But what

During half a century of car production at Munich, a lot of important cars were created by BMW. (BMW)

With 50 years between them, the 502 and E46 Compact are poles apart yet are key players in the BMW story. (BMW)

they did brilliantly was entertain the driver, with perfectly weighted steering and excellent suspension rates. When *Autocar* drove one of the first cars, the verdict was: 'the handling and steering are delightful – you need a closed track to explore the upper limits of cornering behaviour, which is where the old car handled amusingly and safely, even if it tended to break grip at the tail at rather too low a speed.'

The 3-Series was introduced to expand BMW's output significantly, but the company's directors could never have foreseen just how popular the car would be – despite a high price which some found difficult to justify. For certain markets, the price of a 3-Series was

The first-generation 3-Series continued the excellent work done by the '02 series and boosted both BMW's popularity and its profits. (LAT)

The E21 was available in two-door form only – something which restricted sales. BMW would not make this same mistake again. (LAT)

even higher – at £3,429 in the UK in basic 316 form, the cheapest car in the BMW range was more expensive than a Jensen Healey, although at least it was a damn sight more reliable! What was really crazy though was the fact that a pair of Triumph Spitfires could be bought for less than the cost of a 320i; customers had to *really* want one to pay that kind of price. But customers did want the cars badly enough to cough up – in the final full year of production before the arrival of the 3-Series, BMW sold 184,330 cars. Despite the 3-Series not going on sale until July 1975, sales figures for that year leapt to a healthy 221,298. In the first full year of 3-Series production more than 275,000 cars were churned out by BMW and in 1977 the sales tally was in excess of 290,000. It seemed the company could do no wrong as sales increased once more in 1978 (to over 320,000) and by the time the E21 was taken out of production in 1983, a massive 1.36 million had been sold. Of all those examples built, more than half were exported, with the car proving to be particularly popular in the USA – something which was instrumental in building BMW's reputation in this crucial market.

At first, there were just four-cylinder cars available, in 316, 318 and 320 guises. All of them were carburetted, although there was a range-topping 320i on offer which was equipped with Bosch K-Jetronic fuel injection. In September 1977, both the carburetted and fuel-injected 320s were replaced by a single six-cylinder car – the carburetted 320. Then, in February the following year, there was a new range-topper – the 323i which, like the

earlier 320i, was equipped with Bosch fuel injection. Both these six-cylinder cars featured the all-new M60 powerplant, which had been developed specifically for the 3-Series. BMW's existing six-cylinder engine, the M30, was too big to fit into the E21's engine bay and as it was designed for capacities of 2.5–3 litres, it was too powerful for the 3-Series anyway. The 320 offered 122bhp from its 1,991cc engine while there was 143bhp on tap from the 2,315cc unit of the 323i – enough to take the car to 119mph (191kmh). All cars were fitted with a four-speed manual gearbox, although buyers could pay extra for a five-speed Getrag manual transmission – or if they hadn't bought a 316 they could also opt for a three-speed ZF automatic unit.

When *Car* magazine tested the 323i upon its introduction, it was far from unequivocal in its praise for the car. Although it handled well, there were comments about its noisy rear axle, it was generally noisy at speed, it wasn't especially sophisticated and the six-cylinder engine wasn't even as smooth as some other manufacturers' engines with two fewer cylinders. Not only that, but it was costly and the suspension was too soft at the front compared with the rear. But despite all this there was plenty of performance, it was very well put together and the equipment levels were very high – which went some way to justifying the near-£8,000 price tag.

The most desirable and collectable of all the E21 cars was the Baur Cabriolet, which was first seen in 1977. Based on either the 320 or 323i models, this open-topped version of the E21 was officially called the Hardtop-Cabriolet and it was a conversion carried out by Stuttgart-based Karosserie Baur. Using much the same principle as the targa-topped 2002, the Hardtop-Cabriolet featured a removable rigid panel above the two front seats which filled the gap between the windscreen header rail and the roll bar which was fitted just behind the doors. The back of the car was open and to give weather protection there was a canvas hood which could be folded into a recess between the rear seats and the boot. Despite all this work adding significantly to the car's cost, in five years of production around 3,000 examples were sold.

A new dashboard and revised front panel were joined by rear seat belts and improved heating and ventilation for the 1979 3-Series. In the same year a five-speed manual gearbox became available alongside the four-speed manual and three-speed automatic transmissions with which the range had been launched. By 1982, all six-cylinder cars were fitted with these five-ratio gearboxes as standard, while in 1980, the 316's 1.6-litre engine had grown in capacity to become a 1.8-litre unit. In February 1981, a new entry-level 3-Series was launched – the 315. It was not available in all markets, but where it was on sale it offered some buyers the chance to purchase a new BMW rather than a used one. It was powered by a detuned version of the 1.6-litre powerplant which had previously been fitted to the 316, and the model remained in production even for a while after the arrival of the E30.

3-Series take two

With sales averaging over 150,000 a year for the E21, great things were expected of its successor – especially in the lucrative US market which had snapped up BMW's cars with great eagerness. In the event, the E30 was even more successful than the E21, with average sales over its 13-year lifespan of a very healthy 180,000 cars or so annually – which means around 20 per cent more cars were finding owners each year. Development of the E30 had begun in 1976, but it was not until November 1982 that it first went on sale. Initially, it was available only as a two-door saloon, in 316, 318i, 320i and 323i guises. The 316 and 318i used the same 1,776cc powerplant, but in the entry-level car there was a carburettor while the 318i (and all the models above it) were equipped with Bosch electronic fuel injection.

Power outputs ranged from 90bhp to 139bhp with top speeds being 109mph (175kmh) for the 316 and 125mph (201kmh) for the 323i – rather more healthy than the outgoing cars. The new car was very clearly identifiable as a BMW, and there were accusations that the company did not really have much to show for six years of development – or at least not on the outside. But BMW's designers and engineers argued that its customers were very conservative, and they bought the company's vehicles because they liked their understated looks. Not only that, but the identity of the model (and indeed the marque) was very clearly defined by those twin headlamps, kidney grille, kinked rear pillar and the general proportions.

As you would expect, when the E30 was being developed an attempt was made to engineer out the shortcomings of its predecessor. That meant making the handling more predictable, increasing the interior space and reducing the car's weight as far as possible. By using advanced computer-aided design techniques it was possible to shave an average of 40kg off the car and by increasing the wheelbase by 70mm, there was more space available for the occupants – although still not enough. To make it handle more predictably the rear suspension was changed quite radically, with the coil and damper units being mounted separately and the trailing arm mounted at a quite different angle. Combined with wider tracks the handling was more fluid and unless the driver was completely inept, it was much easier to keep the car under control even when cornering hard. Inside there was a facia which set a new standard in clarity and ergonomic excellence – from this point on it was the E30 which set the benchmark in cabin design. In keeping with its executive image there was a lot of technology which filtered down from the more luxurious cars in BMW's range such as the 5-Series and 7-Series. Trip computers were an obvious example, but there was also the availability of anti-lock brakes and the fitment of alloy wheels started to become much more popular with this second generation of 3-Series. All cars were fitted with 14-inch wheels, whereas the previous car had made do with 13-inch items – which now enabled larger, more powerful brakes to be fitted. All models were fitted with disc brakes all round, with six-cylinder cars getting ventilated discs at the front – although later on the 323i was to revert to solid discs.

All this chassis engineering clearly worked because when *Autocar* magazine drove one of the first of the E30 models it reckoned: 'the car could be placed very accurately in corners and held securely on line. Understeer builds up to moderate levels, but this can be moderated by easing off the throttle; snapping the throttle shut in the middle of a fast corner still results in a sharp transition to oversteer, but it's catchable and manageable.' So certainly a vote of confidence from that one magazine, but in the same issue that *Car* magazine introduced its readers to the existence of the new BMW there was also a review of its deadliest rival – the Mercedes 190. Unfortunately for the Munich company, its bitter Stuttgart rival was credited on the front cover to be the 'Merc for the masses' and 'the best small car in the world'. Not ideal when the new 3-Series was going to have to last the best part of a decade and was already outclassed. But then the 190 was not a direct rival at that point because the new 3-Series was available with just two doors. In Spring 1983, a four-door saloon joined the range – designed to compete head on with the Mercedes 190.

The Baur-converted 3-Series had proved popular in E21 form, so it made sense to offer an E30-based conversion. By the end of 1983 the car was being shown and in Spring 1984 the car reached the UK market. As with the previous model the conversion wasn't cheap – it added just over £3,000 to the cost of a new car, meaning the basic 316 was now over £10,000 while a range-topping 323i was a hefty £13,353. The construction of the car was much like before, with a rigid panel above the front seats and a cloth hood that covered the rear seats, and there were quarterlights behind the front side windows. Compared with the fully automated folding roofs of today the operations required to open the car to the elements or to close it all up again were rather long-winded, but the conversion was certainly thorough and effective. But all the work done by Baur to create an open E30 was effectively thrown away when, at the Autumn 1985 Frankfurt Motor Show, BMW showed its own

The first open-topped E30s were conversions by Baur and featured a roll bar behind the front seats. This example has been uprated by MK Motorsport. (LAT)

Within two years of the Baur conversion going on sale, BMW introduced its own convertible, which had been developed in-house. This one has been tweaked by Alpina. (LAT)

convertible, produced in-house and without the rather untidy roll bar of the Baur-converted car. Stylish and classy, the BMW drop-top was an instant success, from the moment it first went on sale in Europe in January 1986. The first examples were sold in the UK in May 1986 and right through to the end of production sales were so good that production could hardly keep up with demand. The reason for the car's success was partly because of the badge that it wore: BMW was already becoming the aspirational marque for many, and even if the car hadn't been that good, it would still have sold in some numbers. But the real reason for the car's popularity was because it wasn't an 'also-ran' – it was beautifully engineered and dynamically superb. Huge attention had been paid to the car's torsional stiffness – chopping the roof off it hadn't led to unacceptable levels of scuttle shake. The car's structure was reinforced thanks to the use of much stiffer sills and a strengthened floorpan which used thicker steel in parts.

The rear seat floorpan was double-skinned and there were extra steel plates incorporated in strategic places. Added to this there was extra reinforcement underneath the dashboard and within the front bulkhead while strengthening bars and stiffening plates were to be found in various parts at the front of the structure.

All the hard work put into stiffening the car's bodyshell certainly paid off, as it meant the convertible possessed the same excellent handling with which the closed cars were blessed. The roof mechanism was also beautifully engineered, with the work having been done by Shaer Waechter of Dusseldorf. BMW had worked with Baur and Karmann to create a solution, but in the end it was this small company in Dusseldorf which had come up with the goods. It was undeniably complex – there were six transverse hood bars and seven sticks on each side which used 28 Teflon-coated bearings between them to work smoothly – but it all worked far better than was expected. Not only did it seal the car from the elements but it also brought new levels of refinement and elegance to the world of open-topped motoring, partly due to the adoption of a triple-layer sandwich-construction hood. Even at relatively high speeds, with the roof in place, the car was surprisingly quiet. Considering the extra weight that the convertibles carried over their closed counterparts, it was surprising that performance wasn't adversely affected more than it was. The six-cylinder cars were relatively untroubled by the extra weight, but the four-cylinder cars introduced in 1990 were less able to shrug it off. But although the build quality, handling and performance all made the car very desirable, perhaps one of the greatest reasons for the car's success – especially in the UK – was that it had few rivals. British new car buyers have always been keen on open-topped cars, and at the time of the E30 convertible's introduction there were no other four-seater drop-tops at similar money, and precious few two-seaters either. If buyers didn't opt for the BMW, there wasn't really anything else.

The 3-Series' main rival was the Mercedes 190, so when a diesel version of that car was introduced, BMW had to match it with an 'oil-burner' of its own. Consequently, in 1985 a pair of four-door six-cylinder diesel saloons joined the range, wearing 324d and 324td badges – the former being a normally aspirated diesel while the latter was equipped with a turbocharger. This was a particularly busy time for BMW, with the September 1985 cover of *Car* magazine proclaiming loudly that there would be no fewer than five new versions of the 3-Series on sale in 1986. Alongside the convertible and diesel there would be the first M3, a four-wheel-drive model and the new range-topping 325i. In this edition of the magazine the oil-burning 190 was tested against the newly launched 324d, and it acquitted itself admirably. Although the Mercedes had more interior space and was better to drive, it was also significantly more expensive and less frugal. On balance it was reckoned that the BMW was the better bet, but it wasn't the diesel E30 which is best remembered – the E30 also introduced the world to the concept of a 3-Series which had been comprehensively reworked by BMW's Motorsport division. This car was the M3, explored more fully in Chapter 4, and as you would expect, it was the most extreme factory version of BMW's baby car. This was BMW's answer to the Cosworth-powered 190E 2.3-16 which had appeared in 1984, and it is probably fair to say that whereas the Mercedes is now largely forgotten, the E30 M3 has become one of the great motoring icons of recent times.

But for extreme rarity matched to strong performance, the 220 or so examples of the South African-built 333i must be the ultimate. It was the

By developing the E30 in all sorts of directions, there was a model for everyone. This front cover of *Car* magazine showed how diverse these variants were.

brainchild of Bernd Pischetschrieder, who at the time was technical director of BMW South Africa. He reckoned the range-topping 323i was a bit tame and claimed that the solution was to fit the big-block six-cylinder engine (from the 7-Series) into the 3-Series. Initially, it was fitted in 3.5-litre form but this was reduced to 3.2 litres when it was discovered that there was no loss of usable performance in the transition. BMW experts Alpina lent a hand to help out with the engineering of such details as the exhaust system and cooling as well as the suspension and wheels. In the event, the car was capable of around 150mph (240kmh) and although it had only 200bhp or so on tap, there was plenty of low-down torque. Although production did not last very long, all cars were fitted with right-hand drive – and a few found their way out of South Africa, but there were one or two that made it to the UK and Hong Kong.

While the 333i was merely a local distraction – back in Europe, BMW was keen to keep an eye on what Audi was up to, as apart from Mercedes, this other German car maker was one of BMW's greatest rivals. Audi had started to build itself a reputation for producing cars which handled well and were very safe because of their technically innovative quattro four-wheel-drive systems. Mercedes had introduced its 4-Matic transmission and while BMW has never managed to build its own reputation for four-wheel-drive innovation in the same way that Audi has, it was with the E30 that BMW decided to start trying to compete. The 325iX which resulted wasn't available for very long in the UK, although it was imported initially – albeit only in left-hand-drive form. After a year the car was withdrawn from the UK market, but by the time E30 production had ended, nearly 30,000 examples had been sold in European and North American markets. In that 1985 edition of *Car* magazine the newly introduced 325iX (the X denoting the fitment of a four-wheel-drive transmission) was pitched against the Audi 90 quattro. Despite Audi's expertise in all-wheel drive, it was considered that the BMW was the better of the two cars – although costing around ten per cent more than its rival, that is perhaps not entirely surprising. This superiority was possibly down to the fact that the transmission was built using various Ferguson patents, that company having worked on four-wheel-drive transmissions since the 1960s. Having championed the cause of rear-wheel drive for many decades, BMW opted for its four-wheel transmission to have a torque split heavily biased towards the back wheels – the final result was a 37:63 front:rear split. With the front wheels having to be driven it was necessary to alter the front suspension to take the necessary hardware – the result was a special subframe on which all the suspension was housed, including the bespoke aluminium lower wishbones. Because there was a lot of extra weight over the equivalent rear-wheel-drive model the X cars were always slower, but the attention to detail paid by BMW meant they were generally not much less entertaining to drive and usually safer into the bargain.

In Autumn 1985, the 3-Series was freshened up with some minor interior and exterior revisions along with a few mechanical changes at the same time. The most prominent external change was the adoption of a slightly tidier nose treatment. Along with the introduction of a small lip spoiler there were fewer bars in the grille and cars without alloy wheels were fitted with a new design of wheel trim. Inside there were more supportive seats and an analogue clock in place of the digital item fitted previously. Stronger steering locks were also introduced and a year later, for the 1987 model year, much of the chrome exterior brightwork was replaced with black anodised trim which looked rather more contemporary. In the same vein, the stainless-steel-finished bumper tops were replaced by colour-coded items – something which had rather more visual impact than it sounds.

For the 1988 model year there was an even bigger change to the 3-Series line up – the re-introduction of the Touring, with the arrival of a new estate car in September 1987 at that month's Frankfurt Motor Show. BMW does not like the term 'estate', but that is exactly what it was, albeit one which put style ahead of function – instead the company called its new baby an 'elegant holdall'. Unlike the earlier car which had used the same name, the new Touring was available as a five-door only, and although space may not have been its strong point, its classy image was perfect for the ambitious, young customers who were flocking to buy it. As with all the other versions of the 3-Series that were available, BMW focused on the car's dynamics, safety and build quality to ensure success. To that end great attention to detail was paid when it came to setting up the suspension along with honing the aerodynamics and obtaining maximum body strength while also achieving the lowest possible weight. Estate cars are notoriously less stiff than their saloon counterparts, so to minimise any loss in torsional rigidity the Touring was fitted with a different design of roof along with much strengthening of the side panels. Even the rear and side windows were bonded to increase stiffness, and sure enough, the work paid dividends with yet more rave reviews. Because the Touring was expected to be something of a load lugger, all models were fitted with disc brakes all round and there was the option of anti-lock technology on all models – except the range-topping 325i on which it was fitted as standard. For buyers who were feeling especially flush, hydropneumatic self-levelling rear suspension was available, and with a maximum payload of just under half a tonne, this could prove to be very useful.

With all these innovations and derivatives successfully introduced with the E30 3-Series, the third-generation car was perfectly placed to pick up the baton and run with it. Buyers would be expecting more variety than ever, which is why BMW would have to engineer four-wheel-drive models, convertibles, estates and an M derivative. Not only would BMW rise to the challenge, but every version of the E36 3-Series would be a huge improvement over its E30 predecessor.

Chapter Two

The third generation – the E36

The arrival of the E36 3-Series in 1990 brought with it a change of direction for BMW with its compact executive. The 3-Series brand was well established by now as it had been around for a decade and a half, and it was firmly established in buyers' minds as a well-built sporting saloon with excellent dynamics if rather spartan equipment levels. Clearly, BMW was keen to maintain the car's reputation as a fine performer, but instead of focusing on the two-door saloon, which was what had been practised with the E21 and E30 derivatives, the company wanted to expand the customer base by concentrating its marketing – and sales – on the four-door saloon. This had come about because of the E30's popularity as a four-door saloon, and the introduction of an E30 Touring had also gone down very well, so to build on that estate's success, the E36 Touring would be marketed far more aggressively.

The convertible E30 had brought open-topped production in-house, and that would continue with the E36, and to reinforce the sporty image that BMW

wanted to portray with its cars, the two-door 3-Series was called a Coupé, on account of it featuring a completely different body from the rest of the family, from the A-pillars back. As if that wasn't enough, later in the model's life a three-door hatch called the Compact would be launched – this is covered more fully in Chapter Five. With so many engine choices and body styles, the third generation of 3-Series couldn't fail but increase sales for BMW.

The change of marketing emphasis for the new 3-Series was not the only shift for BMW, as there was an unfortunate – and unplanned – change of direction. With the E36, BMW began to get a reputation for poor quality products, because of early cars being dogged by problems which are touched on later. Uncharacteristic of BMW it may have been, but there was no denying that the car had not been developed properly before it went on sale.

At first, the third-generation 3-Series was available as a four-door saloon only (328i). (BMW)

Although the E36 was bigger than its predecessor, it still lacked enough cabin space to be truly comfortable. (BMW)

The E36 had started to be developed in the mid-1980s, when the E30 was enjoying particular success. The essential concept of the 3-Series brand had to remain intact for the third-generation model, but the E30's shortcomings had to be addressed if the range was to be expanded successfully. The biggest problem with the second-generation car was its size – it was simply too small to be classed a proper four-seater. That meant not only an increase in external

If front-seat passengers wanted enough space to get themselves comfortable, those behind really struggled to find enough leg room. This is a 318i saloon. (LAT)

dimensions, but better packaging in the cabin. Other areas for improvement included the cars' fuel efficiency, handling, crash safety and running costs. By reducing servicing requirements, the car would be cheaper to run, and with one eye on the environment, the E36 would have to be at least 80 per cent recyclable.

The decision was made from the outset to make the car 110mm longer than the E30, as well as 50mm wider and 10mm taller. To improve rear seat space the wheelbase was extended, but although the wheels were 127mm further apart, rear seat passengers benefited by just an extra 38mm. The E30 had always been criticised for not having enough rear seat legroom and this was BMW's chance to redress the balance. But an inch and a half of extra space for rear seat passengers simply wasn't enough, although the ride did improve thanks to the extended wheelbase, and boot capacity was increased. Much of the extra length had gone into a longer nose, to improve crash safety and adjust the weight distribution. The result of this work was dramatically improved safety levels, with the far stiffer monocoque easily being able to pass the toughest crash tests in the world – the US Federal ones.

To minimise the risk of corrosion in the bodyshell, the new 3-Series featured much-improved rust protection, with a greater use of galvanised panels (66 per cent of the panels were now zinc-coated), and plastic. An extra benefit of the increased use of plastics was a healthy weight saving, which helped the new car to be more fuel efficient than the outgoing model. But the most important characteristic of the E36, in terms of increasing fuel efficiency, was the much more aerodynamic design. By paying close attention to the car's drag factor, the Cd was cut to between 0.29 and 0.32, depending on how highly specified the model was. This improvement was achieved by using faired-in headlamps, an integrated rear spoiler, a more steeply raked windscreen and side glass that was more or less flush fitting. Even the kidney grille was reduced in size and underbody panels to reduce turbulence at speed played their part in ensuring the car cut through the air as efficiently as possible. Such attention to detail meant high-speed stability was greatly improved – front end lift was reduced by 19 per cent and rear end lift cut by 44 per cent.

A perfect weight distribution of 50/50 front to rear helped to ensure safe, predictable handling and a bodyshell that was 45 per cent stiffer than its predecessor's also played a part. To ensure handling was up to the standard expected of a BMW, the suspension was a refined version of what had been fitted to the E30. This development work had certainly paid off, because when the car was first seen, the resulting claim by *Autocar* was: 'The new 3-Series stomps all over the old in terms of roadholding and on the limit handling. Both aspects have been transformed . . . success is absolute'.

Until the advent of the E36, the 3-Series was renowned for having good handling, but could also be a bit ragged on the limit. With the new car, BMW wanted to make the car as enjoyable to drive as possible, but to make its on-limit handling more predictable. That meant MacPherson struts all round were retained on the new car, but anti-roll bars at both the front and rear were fitted as standard on all models. The rear suspension still used trailing arms, but the design was changed comprehensively with a move to a multi-link set-up. This was a development of the 'Z-axle' first seen in the limited-production Z1 of 1986, and the whole lot was polished off with twin-tube gas dampers, which helped to give the car a ride that was better than most of its rivals.

BMW may have slipped up with the packaging, but the new car's dynamics were as good as ever. (BMW)

DID YOU KNOW?

The Z1 was never intended to be a production car – it was built as a test mule for BMW's Z-axle rear suspension. But once it was shown in public with a high-tech bodyshell, the demand was such that leaving it as a one-off made no sense. In the end, 8,000 were made, but with a price in the UK of £37,728, it would never be anything more than a niche model.

The Z1 was not originally intended for production, but demand was such that a limited run was produced by BMW. (BMW)

Rack-and-pinion steering was fitted to all versions of the E36, and except for some examples of the 316i, all cars had power assistance. By assisting the steering it was possible to make it much more direct, which was just as well, because an unassisted 316i had a frankly ridiculous 5.1 turns between locks. As had become standard practice with each successive generation of 3-Series, the wheels gained an inch in diameter for the E36, which meant a minimum of 15in. As well as allowing lower profile tyres, the main benefit of the change was the opportunity to fit larger brakes. Buyers of six-cylinder cars got disc brakes all round whereas drum brakes were fitted to the rear of four-cylinder examples – unless the buyer opted for ABS, in which case the price included an upgrade to disc brakes as well.

By the time of the E36's launch, safety had moved very high up the agenda, and buyers of any car expected to be looked after if the worst happened. But anyone spending their money on a 3-Series expected more than most – buyers of premium cars wanted premium safety levels. The stiffer bodyshell went some way towards providing this, but there were plenty of other features to up the tally, with anti-lock brakes available on some cars, pre-tensioned seatbelts fitted as standard throughout the range and a structure which was claimed to be as strong as a 5-Series in the event of an impact. At low speeds the black bumpers front and rear did an admirable job of bouncing back, but they looked pretty ugly and made the car appear rather cheap. As a result, they did not last long and were soon replaced with colour-coded items which immediately improved the looks of the car.

It was not just the exterior that was much improved over the old model – the interior received a thorough reworking as well. BMW is renowned for its ergonomically sound cabin design, and the E36 took that to new heights. The main instrument binnacle featured a set of four main dials and the centre console was angled towards the driver for the best possible view of the main controls, such as ventilation and the trip computer. The facia was also designed from the outset to offer both driver and passenger airbags, although neither of these was standard on all versions at first and of course, the driver's airbag was housed in the steering wheel rather than the dash itself.

Cloth trim was standard throughout the range, although leather was available for buyers of six-cylinder cars, and for those who really liked to throw the car about – which it did tend to invite – there was a sports seat option offering better lateral support. It was this cloth trim which was to prove to be a major source of headaches for BMW, along with numerous other trim problems. The cloth simply wasn't durable enough, and as a result, interiors were starting to look tatty alarmingly quickly. But the biggest problem was that of low quality plastics being used in the cabin – the dashboard squeaked and rattled as the materials flexed, sunroofs leaked and doors didn't seal properly. The only solution was to have a rapid rethink and upgrade the materials used before BMW lost its hard-won reputation for producing high-quality cars. Stronger, more expensive-looking cloth was used throughout the cabin and quality control on the production line was brought into line with the company's – and customers' – expectations. The plan worked and without too much attention having been drawn to the problems, the car was soon up to BMW's usual standard.

BMW has never been renowned for generous equipment levels, and the E36 was typical of this. Even now, buyers have to spend a significant amount of money when buying a new 3-Series if they want a highly specified car, but when the E36 was launched it came with even less standard equipment than the current cars do. While most buyers wouldn't see this as a good thing, BMW claimed it was in the buyer's interests because they could specify the car how they wanted it. Items such as air conditioning, electric seats, stereo and anti-theft systems could all be specified by the customer, so that they could have the equipment important to them. If they were a non-smoker they could even specify the ashtray delete option, meaning the ashtray, which was normally fitted as standard, was removed. Such personalisation extended beyond equipment, to colour schemes both inside and out. Buyers of six-cylinder cars could choose leather in no fewer than six different colours, while exterior colours ranged through solid and metallic hues to ensure that no two cars to leave the production lines ever needed to be exactly the same.

Although BMW's aim with the E36 was to increase sales significantly, the car was also to take BMW upmarket with higher equipment levels and, consequently, higher prices. The outgoing 316i was priced at around £13,000 whereas the new model was a hefty £14,500, which represented a strong, 11.5 per cent increase. At first, only petrol engines were offered, the choice being between 1,596cc 316i, 1,796cc 318i, 1,991cc 320i and 2,494cc 325i, the first two being four-cylinder units and the other two having six cylinders. They were all fuel-injected and fitted with catalytic converters as standard from the outset, which meant that the E36 was the first range from BMW which ran exclusively on unleaded petrol, although by Summer 1992 – in the UK at least – such equipment was mandatory on all cars anyway.

Of course, it is always nicer to have a six-cylinder engine rather than a mere 'four', but in the case of the first E36 cars, this was especially the case. The initial supply of four-cylinder cars used the eight-valve powerplant carried over from the E30, whereas later cars used a 16-valve unit which was both more powerful and much quieter. When *Autocar* tested an early 318i it was noted that it: 'had neither the performance nor the engine quietness the rest of the car deserves. Eager and smooth but always audible and unpleasantly boomy at motorway speeds, it needs to be worked hard for anything approaching brisk progress.'

Power outputs for these four-cylinder engines were the same as for those in the E30 cars, although their power and torque curves were altered thanks to significant changes to the engine management system, more free-flowing cylinder heads and shorter, lighter pistons which allowed the units to run more smoothly. These engines were part of the M40 family and they

were joined by the rather more appealing six-cylinder M50 powerplants, which were new to the 3-Series. These units had first been fitted to the 5-Series just a few months earlier, and compared with the six-cylinder engines seen in the E30, they gained around 20bhp. Much of this was attributable to the fact that with the previous engines each cylinder had just two valves – the new cars used four-valve heads to allow the engine to breathe more easily. So, whereas the four-cylinder cars were greeted unenthusiastically by *Autocar's* road tester, the six-cylinder car (or at least the 325i) was reviewed rather more positively: 'Performance is excellent but it's the character of the engine that makes a six-cylinder 3 so special. Exquisitely smooth and fine sounding, with a new, more purposeful multi-valve edge, their refinement and exemplary manners, allied to a sweet-shifting gearchange and flawless pedals, contribute much to the driving pleasure BMW talks of so often. The 318i needs more of it.'

The M50 engine was universally praised because of the attention to detail that had been paid in reducing noise levels, increasing refinement and flattening the torque curve. The adoption of chain drive for each of the overhead camshafts improved reliability and made the engine run more quietly. There was fully sequential fuel injection and each combustion chamber had its own ignition coil. Bosch supplied the engine management set-up, which by now had been upgraded to the latest DME 3.1 system and in a bid to keep front-end weight to a minimum, even the inlet manifolds were made of plastic – something which was pioneered with this application, but which in time would become standard on all BMWs. As well as newly fettled engines, the E36 brought with it the option of a five-speed automatic transmission, which was quite a novelty for such a small car. Even luxury cars were still using four-speed autos in the main, so the choice of five ratios was quite a coup for BMW. Available only with the six-cylinder engine, this new transmission was perfectly suited to the powerplant with smooth changes between gears, and a brisk kickdown when rapid acceleration was needed.

DID YOU KNOW?

At the 1994 Detroit Car Engineers' Show a 3-Series was displayed, fitted with a 165bhp two-stroke straight-six engine. Manufactured by Orbital, the four-door saloon featured a 100kg (220lb) all-alloy powerplant and it was hoped that the car would be a production reality within two years. We're still waiting . . .

The first diesels

By Autumn 1991 it was time for the UK-market 3-Series to get its first six-cylinder diesel engine. Left-hand drive markets had been given the option of a 324td, the engine for which had been carried over from the E30, but for the E36, and for right-hand drive markets in particular, BMW was keen to improve on that engine with an all-new unit. It was not going to be all that difficult to improve on this engine because it wasn't exactly cutting edge by the time the new 3-Series had been launched, so British reviewers greeted the new arrival with some anticipation. Developed from the M21 unit, the new arrival was the 2,498cc M51 turbocharged powerplant and it was fitted to the 325td. To maintain its sporty image BMW didn't offer a normally aspirated version, instead choosing to make the car more powerful rather than less.

The result of this thinking was the introduction in 1993 of the intercooled 325tds, which offered 143bhp and 192lb ft of torque compared with 115bhp and 160lb ft for the standard car. Indirect injection had been retained for the engine because it was claimed that such a move would allow it to more easily meet emissions regulations. It was also possible to reduce diesel rattle by adopting a combustion chamber which incorporated a recessed V in the piston crown – something which required the use of a system that allowed the combustion to take place in a swirl chamber connected by a passage to the main combustion chamber.

Unfortunately for BMW, the decision was taken for the intercooled engine to be fitted to the 5-Series (in the 525tds) at the same time that the standard unit was fitted to the 3-Series. Had the 325td been tested in isolation, it would have fared very well. But by giving journalists the opportunity to sample the two engines against each other, the better engine of the two only highlighted the inadequacies of the non-intercooled unit. Although the 325td was a little bit more economical than the bigger and heavier 525tds, it was also rather less powerful: 115bhp against 143bhp. It also had just 164lb ft of torque compared with the 192lb ft of the 525tds. To put the 525tds figure into perspective, with 57bhp per litre, the intercooled engine had the highest specific power output of any diesel engine available anywhere in the world.

After *Autocar* had reviewed the 325td along with the 525tds in the autumn of 1991, and been somewhat equivocal about the smaller of the two cars, there was quite a turnaround in opinions when the 325td was driven against the M3 two years later. This time around the car received such glowing praise that it was as though the piece had been written by BMW's PR team. It contains so many positive quotes that it would be easy to reproduce the whole test here, but suffice to say that the mix of smoothness and refinement, economy, performance and excellent dynamics made the car pretty much unbeatable. In fact, it was claimed that the 325td was so good it was 'enough to steal the M3's thunder'.

With such praise heaped upon the 325td, it doesn't take much to imagine how well the intercooled 325tds was received when it went on sale just a couple of months after *Autocar*'s glowing review of the 325td had been published. The introductory paragraph for *Autocar*'s review of the new arrival said it all: 'Forget petrol. BMW's new diesel sport is faster, more frugal and more desirable.' With a top speed of 134mph (216kmh) and the potential of turning in an average fuel consumption figure of well over 30mpg, it was no surprise that this diesel 3-Series was proclaimed to be not just the best diesel car in the world, but one of the best cars of any type at any price. *Car* was equally positive: 'BMW's six-cylinder engine is the exception that establishes standards by which all Doc Diesel's children must now be judged.'

The Coupé makes its debut

A few months after the first right-hand drive six-cylinder diesel 3-Series had gone on sale, the second – of what would ultimately become four – bodystyles was introduced. Although there had been a two-door version of the E30, it had been marketed as a two-door saloon. BMW decided to play its sporty card with the

Although it wasn't the first six-cylinder turbodiesel 3-Series, the 325tds was the first BMW to have a truly impressive large-capacity oil-burning engine. (LAT)

E36, and the two-door car, introduced in January 1992, was sold as the Coupé. The reality was that it was somewhere between the two, as it had the practicality of a saloon (albeit with a few rear-seat headroom and access sacrifices) while retaining a proper boot. But to ensure its lines were as sleek as possible the roofline was altered quite significantly over the saloon's so that the end result was a car which sat 30mm lower. This was partly thanks to the amended roofline but the bonnet and boot lines were adjusted and so was the rake of both front and rear screens. It wasn't only the height that was unique to the Coupé, as the width was also reduced by 10mm and to finish off the cosmetic differences there was a new set of rear light clusters to give the car a distinctive look from the rear.

Although the rear seat space was compromised, as a two-seat grand tourer the 3-Series Coupé made much more sense because the seat backs could be folded down to give a very generously proportioned load bay. As soon as the new car appeared there were questions as to why BMW hadn't been more adventurous with the styling – if just about every panel had been changed anyway, why not do something more radical and create a car with a true coupé profile? The simple answer was that BMW felt it did not want to experiment too much with its very successful 3-Series formula, and with a large proportion of Coupés expected to go to business users, it wouldn't do to discourage them by offering something that was impractical for everyday use.

From the outset, the Coupé was available with a choice of three engines. The entry-level car was the

When the two-door E36 was launched in 1992, it was marketed very differently from the E30 because it was known as the Coupé; this is a 323i. (BMW)

1,796cc 318iS, which took the eight-valve engine fitted to the 318i and replaced it with a new powerplant which was a development of the unit that had been fitted to the E30 318iS. Part of the M42 family of engines, the new unit wasn't – on paper – that much of an advance over the engine seen in the E30. It offered 140bhp against the previous car's 136bhp, but that was only part of the story. BMW had fitted the unit with a variable-length intake manifold to flatten the torque curve but if there still wasn't enough power and torque on offer the buyer could opt for a six-cylinder engine. In fact, there was a choice of two six-cylinder

The dash of the Coupé would be familiar to any E36 driver – it was one of the best facias around, as on this 328i. (LAT)

The cabin of the Coupé (328i) was also on a par with other E36 models produced by BMW, with supportive seats and excellent ergonomics. (LAT)

Not so great was the amount of space available for those who had to sit in the back of this 323i Coupé, but for small people it was very comfortable! (LAT)

powerplants: the 1,991cc 320i or the 2,494cc 325i. They were both 24-valve units and offered 150bhp and 192bhp respectively – plus of course the smoothness that was inherent in the BMW six-pot engine.

The Coupé was a strong advocate of the 'less is more' school of thought, although not everybody believed the hype. The car was priced at quite a premium over its four-door stablemates – the top models were up to £2,000 more expensive – and there were some who felt that the price hike wasn't justified. After all, the car offered less rear headroom and despite the rather longer doors, less convenient access to those seats. But

Many years after its introduction, the E36 Coupé still looks classy, with its svelte lines and a hint of effortless power; this is a 328i. (LAT)

of course, those buying the Coupé were unlikely to be bothered by such matters and BMW could justify the higher prices by offering higher levels of equipment as standard. As well as anti-lock brakes being standard for all derivatives, there was M-Technic suspension (which was a delete option), electric windows and alloy wheels all included in the price. Because there were no weight penalties for the Coupé over the saloon, performance figures weren't compromised and because there were few changes over the four-door car, the excellent driving characteristics of that car were retained. *Car* magazine claimed it was even better than that – at least in six-cylinder guise – with the car being more fun to drive than BMW's range-topping 850i, a car which cost around three times as much.

Not long after *Car* magazine had performed its test of the 325i Coupé, in September 1992, BMW introduced its VANOS variable valve timing system on all the M50 (six-cylinder) powerplants – a technology which quickly filtered through to all the company's petrol engines. It wasn't the first time this technology had been available to 3-Series buyers, as it had been fitted to the M3 and was a standard feature on Motorsport-developed engines. By moving the camshafts backwards or forwards hydraulically, the valve timing could be optimised to give both low-end torque and top-end power – something which previously had to be compromised in favour of one or the other. Needless to say, it made an already excellent engine even better, with torque not having to be sacrificed at low engine speeds, but extra power was available higher up the rev range. Despite the Coupé being raved about by all who drove it, things were to get even more stylish for drivers who wanted a 3-Series with a bit of extra flair.

Introduction of the Convertible

From the moment the sleekly styled Coupé was first seen, it was obvious that the car would make the perfect basis for a drophead 3-Series. Of course BMW hadn't been stupid, and such a car was in the company's model plans and by Summer 1993 the first production E36 Convertible was on display. The car had been designed and engineered in-house, as BMW was no longer dependent on outside help as it had been with the E21. The E30 Convertible, which had remained on sale long after the E36 saloon had become available, had been developed in-house. And just like that car, the new model carried with it a significant weight penalty over its four-door saloon counterpart. The E30 Convertible had weighed 131kg (289lb) more than the closed car and BMW was keen to reduce this as much as possible. In the event, the weight penalty was still a hefty 120kg (265lb), which did little to help the car's performance figures, but the pay off was that the

DID YOU KNOW?

Although BMW built the E36 convertible in-house, having ditched the Baur-built dropheads seen with the earlier 3-Series, it was still possible to buy a Baur-converted E36 cabriolet. Based on the four-door saloon – and hence available with any engine – the Baur E36 Topcabriolet offered a peel-back roof while retaining the side profile of the standard car.

The Coupé may have turned the E36 into a sports car, but the Convertible made it a real head-turner. (BMW)

stiffness of the bodyshell ensured scuttle shake wasn't an issue. The bodyshell of the Convertible had rather more in common with the Coupé than it did with the saloon, with the steeply raked windscreen, a pair of very long doors and (with the roof up) the same basic profile.

In keeping with the premium image of the Convertible, the folding roof was a substantial affair that was beautifully engineered. On most cars it was power-operated, but some entry-level cars were specified with manual mechanisms. With typical BMW attention to detail the folding roof was part of an integrated package that saw all four side windows lowered when the roof was retracted or raised. Once the roof had been stowed or raised the windows would then be raised once more – the whole system was a work of art. Although there was no fixed roll bar behind the seats, provision had been made should the car become accidentally inverted. The first line of defence was a massively strengthened windscreen surround, which BMW claimed was capable of taking most of the strain in the event of a rollover. But it didn't have to do all the work as there was a pair of roll bars located behind the rear seats which popped up as soon as sensors detected something was wrong. The result of all this work was a car which BMW claimed would be able to support a 316 saloon without the windscreen surround buckling and as well as easily passing the US rollover regulations, it was also claimed that the Convertible was able to pass the even more stringent rules which applied to saloons.

UK buyers were able to get their hands on the 3-Series Convertible from August 1993, and at first only the range-topping 325i was on offer. By this stage more than half a million examples of the E36 had rolled off BMW's production lines, and with only the saloon and Coupé version available until this time, the introduction of the Convertible could only see even more 3-Series finding buyers. The 3-Series was enjoying unshakeable popularity – the huge premiums demanded for the Convertible made no difference to demand and buyers couldn't get enough. The 325i Convertible, without any extras, cost a hefty £28,000. That was a £6,000 – or 21 per cent – premium over its nearest and most obvious rival, the Audi Cabriolet. By the time the optional body-coloured aluminium hard top had been specified for £2,000, or the electrically adjustable heated leather seats were chosen from the options list, the car's price had escalated to well over £30,000. But it made no difference – everyone who reviewed the car said it was

After the E30, the E36 was the second drop-top 3-Series built in-house by BMW – and the roof mechanism worked beautifully, as on this 325i. (LAT)

worth the money. It wasn't just about how good the BMW was, it was also about the fact that there was no credible competition. Audi's Cabriolet was antiquated and so was Saab's 900. It wasn't so much that the BMW was expensive as the alternatives were cheaper because the cars simply weren't anything like as good.

These rival manufacturers also did not offer anything like the number of opportunities to personalise the car that BMW did – not only because of an extensive options list but because with the 3-Series Convertible, the decision was taken to launch the Personal Line. This was a scheme whereby those who bought a drop-top 3-Series were able to specify whatever they wanted in terms of interior or exterior colours, and no matter how broad the standard colour chart was, there would always be buyers who wanted something that nobody else had got.

The reasons for the eulogies to the Convertible were manifold, but centred on the exquisite engineering of the whole car and the fact that dynamic ability wasn't really compromised by the lack of a roof. Few cars could claim to be just about every bit as good as the saloon or coupé on which they were based – the fact that this convertible had been planned as a model in its own right rather than merely a converted coupé showed through very clearly. BMW claimed that the Convertible was at least 90 per cent as stiff as the Coupé, which itself was 30 per cent

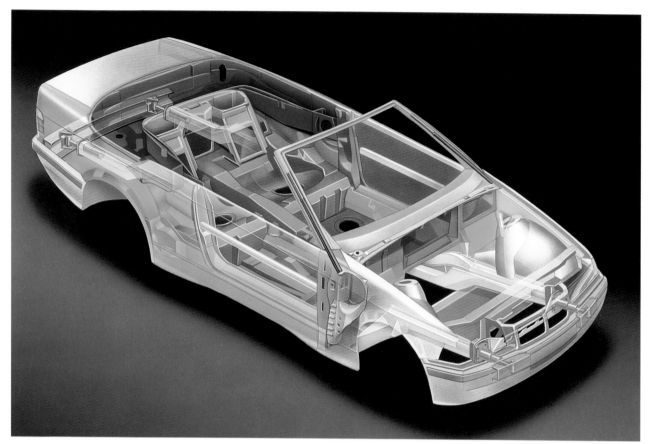

Above: Safety wasn't overlooked, with the Convertible's structure massively reinforced to ensure crash stiffness. (BMW)

Below: The strengthened bodyshell also went some way towards ensuring excellent dynamics with very little scuttle shake. (BMW)

DID YOU KNOW?

BMW built a diesel-powered E36 convertible, although the car remained a one-off. It was produced by BMW Individual, the company's in-house personalisation outfit and although the car was available to special order, there was little point in buying it in place of a regular petrol-powered convertible. The car was based on the 325tds and although it was 100kg (220lb) heavier than the saloon counterpart, the drop-top still had strong performance and low noise levels once it was moving.

stiffer than its predecessor. Whether the roof was up or down the car's lines were clean and elegant and apart from the high price, the only criticism levelled against the car was the fact that rear seat legroom was compromised a bit too much because of space having to be found for the roof when stowed.

Although performance was marginally less sparkling than with the closed car, it made little difference because there was still a top speed of 142mph (228kmh) on offer, along with the possibility of covering the 0–60mph (96kmh) dash in just 8.6 seconds – hardly sluggish. Refinement was also very good and with the roof up, at normal cruising speeds, the interior noise levels were barely any higher than in the closed cars. With the roof down and the side windows up it was equally comfortable once cruising and as long as there were no rear seat occupants, it was possible to install an anti-buffeting mesh screen which reduced turbulence within the cabin to the point where it was hardly any more breezy than in a closed car with the window down. Having said that, it is all very well reducing turbulence and noise to closed car levels, but doesn't that defeat the object of buying an open-topped car in the first place?

Selling only the range-topping Convertible was all well and good, but there were a lot of potential buyers out there who wanted a drophead 3-Series and who were either unable or unwilling to spend so much money. Fortunately, BMW realised a cheaper option had to be offered so the 318i and 320i Convertibles were introduced in Summer 1994. Costing £22,410 and £23,980 respectively, both did without power-operated folding roofs although for an extra £700 one could be specified. When *Top Gear* magazine reviewed a 320i Convertible the judgment was as positive as ever, although the tester did claim there was noticeable scuttle shake. Like its bigger brother, the 320i Convertible had no shortage of refinement – although there was a predictable performance cut thanks to just 150bhp being offered by the 2.0-litre straight-six. But

that reduction in urge was rather less than the 318i Convertible's which also couldn't claim the same levels of smoothness or refinement on account of a four-cylinder engine being fitted. This was the same 16-valve engine that was normally found at the front of the 318iS, which meant its 115bhp was enough to give the car a top speed of 121mph (195kmh) – more than enough for most UK buyers even if the acceleration was rather laid back compared with that of the six-cylinder cars.

The Touring arrives

After the Compact had been introduced in 1994 (covered separately in Chapter Five), the final E36 bodystyle was released in Summer 1995 – the Touring. The name recalled the classic three-door sports estates of the 1960s and '70s, which had not been a great success for BMW, and which is why they weren't replaced when the E21 was introduced. Unlike the previous Touring, the new car was available as a five-door estate only – except BMW went to great lengths to argue that the Touring was not an estate. The reasoning behind this assertion was the fact that in the minds of car buyers, an estate was a practical load lugger whereas BMW's Touring was a car for the sporting driver who happened to need the extra carrying capacity over a saloon. But times have changed and with sporting estates now available from several manufacturers, it is generally accepted (at least outside BMW) that all versions of the Touring are nothing more than estate cars.

The biggest-selling E36 models were those with four-cylinder engines, but the six-cylinder cars were far more impressive to drive, like this 328i Touring. (LAT)

The last E36 derivative to be introduced was the Touring, which may have been more spacious than the other models, but it still put style before practicality; this is a 320i. (LAT)

Despite the lack of success of the original Touring, the E36 model wasn't the first five-door Touring as there had been an E30 version, but this had been discontinued in 1994. From the start of the E36 project it was envisaged there would be an 'estate' offered, so not only were the car's lines very smooth, but the interior space utilisation was also much better than that of the outgoing car. An increase in luggage bay width from 550mm to 889mm meant the space was far more usable, and the split folding rear seats made it even easier to use that space – but still it put style before function. Unbelievably, with the rear seats up, the luggage space available (368 litres) was actually 15 per cent *less* than that of the saloon, but as Georg Kacher wrote in *Car* magazine at the time of the Touring's launch: 'It's not cubic feet and payload that the car's buyers are interested in – it's prestige and lifestyle.'

At first, the Touring was available with a choice of three engines and were designated: 318tds, 320i and

328i. Within a year the highly acclaimed 325tds had joined the range along with a new entry-level version: the 318i. Everybody who reviewed the cars agreed that they were great to drive, had bags of style, and were probably overpriced. And thanks to intrusive rear suspension turrets, the verdict was also unanimous that practicality had almost certainly been sacrificed a bit too much in the pursuit of style. But as was typical with BMW – and still is – everybody agreed that the buyer of the Touring wasn't going to care – they were making a statement, not looking for the last word in carrying capacity. When *Autocar* tested a 320i Touring there could be no denying that other cars did certain things better – Ford's 24-valve Mondeo estate was quicker, cheaper and more capacious than the BMW. Yet it was still easy to recommend the Touring because of the driving experience, and as the tester put it, if you were going to be looking at buying a 3-Series saloon anyway, the Touring would make a very nice alternative. Sure, so the Touring cost more than the saloon, but all five-door 3-Series were equipped to SE spec, which meant the equipment count automatically went up anyway. By the time that was taken into account, there was only £600 in it – no wonder style-conscious buyers queued up to buy them.

Soon after the Touring was first launched, BMW

DID YOU KNOW?

BMW's E30 Touring, introduced in Summer 1987, was not the first 3-Series estate, although it was the first factory-built one. A year before its introduction, the Dutch coachbuilding firm of Luchjenbroers introduced a three-door estate version of the 3-Series. Priced at £3,500 for the conversion alone, when a standard 320i cost £10,250, it is no surprise that very few appear to have been built.

The compact dimensions of the Touring made it wieldy – so much so that it was as good to drive as its E36 stablemates – here is a 328i. (LAT)

revived another classic designation – the 323i. Harking back to the E21 3-Series, and the performance version of that car, the new 323i was fitted with a 2.5-litre engine that produced 170bhp and 181lb ft of torque. The

One of the reasons for the huge desirability of the 3-Series was the excellent range of powerplants. This is the six-cylinder M52 unit, which was seen in the 320i, 323i and 328i. (BMW)

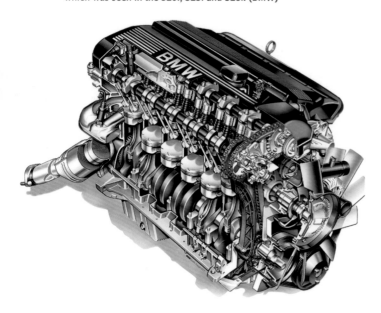

reason the car wasn't badged the 325i was to distance it from the previous 12-valve engine that had been fitted to the E36. The new car had an aluminium cylinder block in place of the previous cast iron unit and was equipped with VANOS and 24 valves, so it was much more sophisticated than the outgoing powerplant. Initially, the engine was fitted to the Coupé only, but it soon filtered down to the rest of the 3-Series range to offer a cheaper six-cylinder alternative to the 328i.

Once all the different bodystyles had been launched, it was time for the whole 3-Series range to be freshened up with revisions to the styling, engines and specifications. That revamp came in 1996, for the 1997 model year. The new 3-Series was still at least two years away – and for some of the bodystyles, rather more than that. In typical BMW fashion the changes were so subtle that few people would have noticed them. The chrome around the double-kidney grille was made marginally thicker and there were some specification changes to keep the car competitive with models that had been introduced since the E36 had first been seen. But even with the old and new cars side by side, you would be hard pressed to spot the change. Still, it didn't matter, because BMW could sell every car it could make – and that didn't change even when the E46 was first shown and some of the E36 models remained in production as the various new bodystyles were introduced over time.

Chapter Three

The fourth generation – the E46

When the fourth-generation 3-Series was launched, its predecessor was somewhat long in the tooth. Although that car had been a huge advance over the E30, by the time it was replaced it had become increasingly outdated in many ways. When *Autocar* had reviewed one of the first examples of the E36 325i, its parting shot was to say: 'The new 3-Series is a winner . . . offering spectacular leaps over the outgoing model . . . But in playing to others' rules BMW has introduced a touch of any-car ordinariness where before there was a more distinct if sometimes flawed personality. It's a good car, but only time will tell if it's a great BMW.'

So, with such equivocal praise, it was obvious there was scope for improvements to be made, even when the E36 was new. Eight years later, when it was finally replaced, those issues had to be addressed as well as keeping pace with (and it could be argued, keeping ahead of) developments seen elsewhere in the marketplace. As well as offering peerless build quality, the new 3-Series had to offer superb dynamics, higher equipment levels, greater safety and cleaner engines. At least BMW, and the 3-Series in particular, had an enviable reputation and was seen as the aspirational car of choice for any image-conscious driver. Despite the shortcomings of the E36, and although BMW works on an eight-year lifecycle for its cars, the company claimed the car could have remained on sale for another two or three years, such was the demand for it.

Although the new car was improved in just about every respect as far as the buyer was concerned, its release was also good news for BMW. Not only did the cost of production of each car fall by 20 per cent, but the assembly time required for each example fell by the same amount. With the 3-Series being by far the biggest seller in the BMW range, that by itself went a fair way to explaining the company's industry-beating profitability.

And by manufacturing the 3-Series in four plants globally (Munich, Dingolfing and Regensburg in Germany as well as a factory in South Africa) the economies of scale could be increased even further.

By the time the E46 was introduced at the 1997 Geneva Motor Show, the popularity of the 3-Series was unassailable. It seemed everyone aspired to owning BMW's compact executive, even if it was only a lowly, four-cylinder example, and the arrival of an all-new model only reinforced this. Just like the E30 and E36, the E46 would take the best elements of the 3-Series and build on them to produce an even more focused car that combined great dynamics with excellent build quality and better packaging. The increase in size of the E36 over the E30 had been welcome, but it hadn't gone far enough towards addressing the problem of space for rear seat passengers – with the E46 this problem would have to be solved once and for all. The result was a car which was 38mm longer, 25mm of which was in the

The model development of the E46 mirrored that of the E36, with only the saloon being available at first (318i). (BMW)

In common with all BMWs, the third-generation 3-Series retained rear-wheel drive. Few of its rivals could claim this, and it set the car apart dynamically. (BMW)

wheelbase. The width increased by 41mm and the height also grew by 22mm. All these combined to produce a car with more leg and head room as well as a greater girth for more shoulder space. Although the increased dimensions meant the weight of the car went up, it also resulted in the wider track allowing the car to corner with greater stability.

Also in common with the rest of the models in BMW's range, the 3-Series had class-leading ergonomics with a superbly laid out facia. (BMW)

The dimensional increases prompted claims that the 3-Series was no longer the compact executive that it started out as, and that perhaps it should no longer wear the familiar badge. But the reality was that the E46 was just 120mm longer than the first of the breed and was still a healthy 300mm shorter than the 5-Series – which of course had also grown along the way. Around the time the first 3-Series appeared, Ford was launching the Fiesta and VW its Golf. Those had also evolved and along the way had grown to the point where they were really a class up from where they began, but they were still deserving of the badges they wore because buyers' expectations had shifted, and they wanted a lot more by the time the E46 was introduced. The new bodyshell brought significant advantages, not least the fact that torsionally it was 70 per cent stiffer than the outgoing car, allowing sharper handling thanks to more precise (and more importantly, consistently precise) suspension location. The floorpan revisions allowed for the front wheels to be moved further forward and because the engine was positioned further back, the weight distribution was more or less ideal at 50:50 front to rear. The fact that rear-wheel drive was retained also allowed excellent driving characteristics with no chance of torque steer even when large, incredibly powerful engines were fitted and there was also the opportunity to tune the car with some extremely powerful engines without having to worry about such a problem.

The E36 had been in production for seven years, and to ensure that the E46 wasn't seen as merely a development of its predecessor, but rather a replacement for it, all parts had to be new – BMW claiming this was the case with the only exception being the sump plug! This meant a new range of powerplants had to be provided, although in reality they were in some cases based heavily on the engines seen in the E36. The new car, which was initially launched in just four-door saloon form, had started life at the end of 1993. As had become common practice with BMW, this was the core product and the other bodystyles would be released at the rate of one a year to allow plenty of time to develop them. In the meantime, the Coupé, Convertible, Touring and Compact versions of the E36 continued to be sold alongside the new saloon.

While the E46 was being developed it had been photographed wearing various disguises, but the essential elements were so typical of the BMW look that nobody was fooled. The hockey stick C-pillar was there, just like it had been for decades and the corporate nose was in evidence, with the pair of kidney grilles that had become a trademark in the 1930s. Although the glassed-in headlamps had become a BMW trademark with the previous 3-Series, for the E46 there was a small pair of scallops cut out of the base of the glass panel to give it a bit more character. The E39 5-Series, which, like the E46 3-Series was a fourth-generation car, had first been seen in 1995. This shared much detail design with its smaller brother including the L-shaped rear lights and coupé-like rear window angle which allowed a high back end to improve aerodynamics and increase boot space.

Safety sells

When the first 3-Series had gone on sale in the 1970s, safety was becoming increasingly important as a selling point. Safety vehicles were all the rage at the start of that decade, and by the time development work for the E46 had got underway, occupant protection was fighting for one of the top slots along with low emissions and strong reliability. As a result, the E46's design incorporated more active and passive safety features than any small car BMW had ever made. Essentially a passive safety system allows a driver to avoid an accident whereas an active safety feature minimises the risk of injury if the worst should happen. To help increase the strength of the car's shell, a large proportion of it incorporated the use of high strength steel in its manufacture.

Massive attention to detail was paid to ensure the E46 was able to stand up to all but the worst impacts. (BMW)

Huge amounts of work, much of it involving computer-aided design techniques, allowed the crumple zones front and rear to be optimised to the point where the new car was 60 per cent stiffer than the old, reducing the chances of intrusion into the passenger cell in the event of a collision. Indeed, such were the advances that had been made, BMW claimed that compared with the E30 of a decade earlier, the E46 was able to absorb two and a half times as much energy before the passenger cell was deformed. Even the E36 that the new car replaced had been nothing like as safe – the E46 was able to absorb 80 per cent more energy in a 40mph (64kmh) impact with a 40 per cent offset barrier.

Around the time that the E46 was introduced, attention had turned to side impact protection. Such accidents were becoming more frequent – or at least they were becoming increasingly prominent because, although they accounted for just 20 per cent of accidents, they were responsible for about 40 per cent of fatalities. Car makers were trying to address the problem by fitting their cars with beams across the doors to reduce the damage caused by side impacts, and this was the case for the E46. Both front and rear doors were equipped with interlocking diagonal bars and the sills were also strengthened to disperse the collision energy throughout the monocoque. Helping the new 3-Series to maintain its place as one of the most technologically advanced – and safe – premium small cars, a whole host of other passive safety features were fitted. Even the cheapest 3-Series was fitted with six airbags as standard, all of which were for front seat passengers. As well as front airbags there was a side air bag in both front doors and another mounted on the B-posts to protect each person at head height. Rear seat passengers could also benefit from door-mounted airbags if the £250 option was specified. A sensor ensured that if there was nobody sitting in the passenger seat, the three airbags on that side would not be activated. Although the saloon was officially a five-seater, there were only three-point seat belts for four, the central rear seat passenger having to make do with a lap belt only.

Active safety features fitted to the new 3-Series were heavily reliant on electronics – computers were not only able to sense and react to danger faster than the average driver, but with sensors mounted all over the car, a central computer could also monitor far more at any one time than the typical driver. So, although a lot of electronic aids had been available on the previous 3-Series – especially towards the end of the model's life – in the new car they were not only more numerous, but also more available due to them filtering into the cheaper (and hence more common) models.

Thanks to the silicon chip, it was possible to equip the 3-Series with such features as anti-lock brakes (ABS), traction control (or ASC+T for automatic stability

If the worst did happen, there were up to eight airbags available to protect the car's occupants – although not all of these were fitted as standard of course. (BMW)

control and traction in BMW-speak), cornering brake control (CBC) and dynamic stability control (DSC). Cornering brake control, or at least something similar, had been seen before, but not in a car the size of the 3-Series. This technology prevented the car from oversteering or sliding while braking on the limits of traction. It worked through the ABS sensors, which detected transverse acceleration and boosted brake pressure at the front to correct the oversteer. The dynamic stability control was available on the range-topping 328i, and because it was the third generation of this type of technology it was known as DSC III. Although it worked much like the CBC fitted to other cars in the range, in the 328i engine power was also reduced and brakes at any of the car's four corners could be applied to limit any deviation from the planned trajectory.

Equipment

Although BMW has always had a reputation for being less than generous with its equipment levels, the reality is that often rather more than just the essential features are fitted as standard. But BMW was clearly sensitive to the criticisms levelled against it regarding equipment levels because in the press pack handed out to journalists at the car's launch, nearly a whole page was devoted to trying to defend the company's position. BMW had always taken the line that it had allowed customers to tailor their cars to suit their own

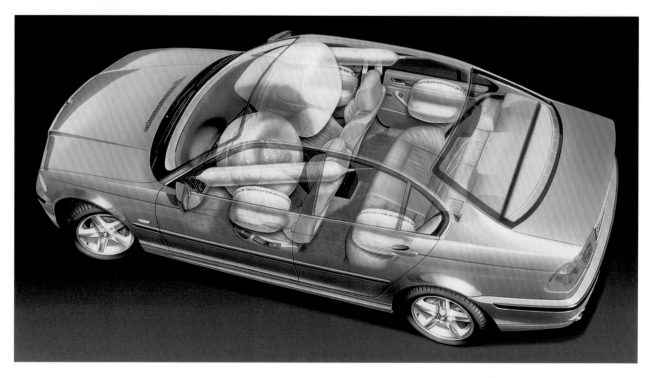

The new model was also as recyclable as possible – shown here are the components fitted which could be recycled when the car's life was over. (BMW)

requirements and with the E46 it was no different. Indeed, when the E46 was launched, it was usual for the press cars to be equipped with nearly £7,000 worth of extras. The line taken was that when a car was reviewed by the press, they should also get the chance to try out some of the options that could be specified – especially worthwhile when it is considered that virtually nobody ever specifies a BMW without at least one or two extra-cost options. But owners didn't have to pay extra for *all* those little luxuries that make living with a car every day that bit nicer, and to demonstrate that BMW could be as over the top as any rival maker of luxury cars, there was what the company called car memory and key memory. Fitted as standard, the former allowed owners to set their own settings for central locking, lighting and air conditioning. The latter option meant up to four key holders could tailor their requirements with respect to electric seat adjustment and central locking functions (ie which doors were unlocked when the key was pressed). It may have seemed a bit flash, but how many owners realised this was possible, never mind actually bothered to set it all up?

Some of the options that could be specified included tyre pressure sensors, which monitored each of the four tyres and notified the driver of any loss of pressure. But having driven a 2003 model year 330d press car, I can vouch for the fact that even in the 21st century, and even on a BMW, the technology isn't fail-safe. Once the warning appears it is only natural to stop at the earliest opportunity to sort out the problem – and it is incredibly annoying to find there isn't one! Owners who

had deep pockets could spend what seemed like a limitless amount on extras, some of which were:

- Integrated rear child seats
- Xenon headlamps
- Multi-media system with satellite navigation
- Parking sensors
- Infrared reflecting windscreen to reduce cabin temperatures
- Multi-function steering wheel to control stereo, telephone and cruise control
- Rain-sensing wipers (standard on 328i SE)
- Uprated stereo choices

The problem with focusing on toys that the owner can see – such as sunroofs, stereos and gadgets for the cabin – is that under the skin things tend to get skimped on. BMW had always taken the opposite approach, preferring instead to engineer its cars well beyond what its rivals felt was necessary, and the company was clearly correct in its approach because compared with other mass-market cars the products of BMW enjoyed pretty much an unrivalled status. The E46 did nothing to change that, with a chassis that was everything a 3-Series buyer had come to expect, many of the lessons learned in the all-new 5-Series (E39) of two years earlier being incorporated into the design of the new 3-Series.

One of the innovations introduced with the E39 was aluminium suspension components to reduce unsprung weight which helped to sharpen handling and improve the ride quality. Rear-wheel drive was retained, which was essential as the same floorpan was to be used for the E46 M3, which was due to make its debut in 2000.

Engines

To take advantage of such a finely honed chassis, a decent range of powerplants had to be offered, and on this score BMW didn't fail to deliver. Although some of the engines were derived from units seen before, BMW had pulled out all the stops to introduce a range of units that could justifiably claim to be new.

Starting off the range was the 318i, which retained nothing more than the name from its predecessor. In place of the old 1.8-litre engine there was a 1.9-litre unit (with a displacement of 1,895cc), which was the first BMW powerplant to be fitted with balancer shafts. Other makers had fitted them before (most notably Mitsubishi and Porsche) to improve refinement and in the 318i it was claimed they reduced noise levels by up to 10dBA – a considerable improvement. The 1.9-litre engine retained just a pair of valves for each cylinder, but it laid claim to having the highest specific torque output (torque per litre) of any two-valve engine in the world, with 70lb ft/litre. More importantly, the engine

The most important engine for mass-market sales was the M43 engine, fitted to the 318i and 316i. (BMW)

had a flat torque curve and although the 118bhp power output was only 3bhp up on the old model, in reality the engine was much more responsive throughout the rev range. Maximum power was generated at 5,500rpm and a seven per cent increase in peak torque meant there was 133lb ft at the driver's disposal, from 3,900rpm.

These improvements in power and torque meant the new 318i was both quicker and more economical than the car it replaced. It could sprint from 0–62mph (100kmh) in 10.2 seconds and hit a top speed of 128mph (206kmh), while the in-gear times were also cut. But despite this better performance, fuel consumption was cut to 35.8mpg, in part thanks to great attention to detail having been paid to reducing friction within the engine. Although the pair of balancer shafts added 8kg (17.6lb) to the engine's mass, weight was shed elsewhere so that overall there was no increase in the weight of the powerplant. All this meant that emissions were reduced – new legislation would be introduced in 2000 with which BMW had to comply. Dubbed EU3 (for the third generation of EU-wide emissions regulations), the rules were much stricter than the EU2 set with which the cars had previously had to comply. To ensure that the 318i wouldn't be hampered by the new limits, a new type of catalytic converter was introduced along with a new computer to monitor all the engine processes. Called the BMS46 control system, the fuelling and ignition were taken care of alongside the adjustment of the variable-length intake manifold together with the temperature of the coolant. By running the engine at higher temperatures it was possible to improve efficiency even further.

At first, the 318i was the only four-cylinder E46 available, but at the February 1999 Amsterdam Motor Show another was introduced: the 316i. Using the same 1,895cc M43 engine as the 318i, the new car featured a lower state of tune due to different camshafts and remapped ignition and in place of the 118bhp of the 318i, there was just 105bhp. But just like the more powerfully tuned powerplant, there was plenty of refinement thanks to the same counter-rotating balancer shafts. Meanwhile, for those who felt that four cylinders weren't enough there was a choice of two cars featuring an extra pair: the 323i and 328i, both of which used the M52 six-cylinder powerplant. Featuring Double-VANOS variable valve timing, both these engines were derived from the one fitted to the previous-generation M3, which meant plenty of torque low down in the rev range and the smoothness that could be taken for granted with any six-pot BMW. Although BMW had tended to name its cars according to the capacity of the engine under the bonnet, the introduction of the E46 discarded that. The 318i used a 1.9-litre engine (as did the 316i) and under the bonnet of the 323i sat a 2.5-litre powerplant pushing out 170bhp at 5,500rpm and 181lb ft at 3,500rpm. At least the 328i housed a 2.8-litre engine, so there was still some predictability, and in the E46 it produced 193bhp at 5,500rpm, with peak torque being 206lb ft at 3,500rpm.

BMW had built a reputation for producing incredibly smooth straight-six engines, and the units installed in the E46 were no exception. At a time when virtually every other manufacturer had moved to more compact V6 designs, BMW stuck with its in-line configuration because of the inherent increase in refinement. With such a layout it would also have been very easy for the cars to be nose-heavy, but thanks to the all-aluminium construction of the units, weight was kept to a minimum. Weighing in at 150kg (331lb) each, the engines could claim to be among the most efficient in their class – BMW stating that within their capacity ranges each powerplant provided the best solution in terms of weight, size, performance, consumption, emissions and refinement. No wonder the cars were always liked by those who reviewed them!

The Double-VANOS system fitted to both six-pots was something of a *tour de force*, allowing torque to be increased at lower engine speeds while power was improved higher up the rev range. But at the same time, fuel consumption was reduced and so were both emissions and engine noise. All this was brought about by advancing or retarding the opening and closing points for the inlet and exhaust valves according to engine speed and load. In common with the 318i's engine, the six-cylinder powerplants also featured a variable length inlet manifold to optimise torque at low revs. The benefits of the system did not stop there as the Resonance Intake System, as it was called, also reduced fuel consumption and emissions at the same time. Meanwhile, even the throttle for the fuel injection was scrutinised and the result was an electro-mechanical system that could be linked to the traction control. Alongside increased smoothness, there was the added benefit of better fuel economy thanks to the throttle position being optimised at all times.

Diesel engines were an important part of the E36 range and with oil-burning cars becoming increasingly

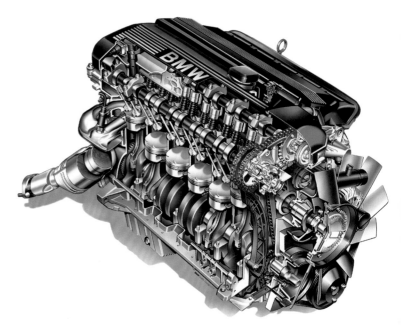

The six-cylinder engines were fitted with Double-VANOS, as pioneered in the E36 M3. This increased low-end torque and high-end power without sacrificing economy. (BMW)

popular across Europe (although Britain was slow to catch on) it made no sense to omit them from the new line up. At first there wasn't a diesel E46, but from Spring 1998 a four-cylinder diesel became available in the form of the 320d. With 16 valves, a turbocharger with intercooler and direct injection, there was no shortage of power or torque. In fact, this engine could lay claim to having the highest specific power and

The E36 325tds had been a great diesel, but BMW moved the game on with the launch of the four-cylinder 320d. (BMW)

torque figures of any diesel car, with 136bhp and 206lb ft on tap – which equated to 68bhp/litre and 103lb ft/litre. This torque figure was the equal of the 328i, but unlike that engine, and thanks to two-phase fuel injection along with a variable nozzle turbine turbocharger, the diesel powerplant could claim to achieve just short of 50mpg – a figure that 328i drivers could only dream of. As a result of this power and torque, the 320d was capable of dismissing the 0–62mph sprint in just 9.9 seconds before topping out at 128mph (206kmh) – four seconds and 19mph (31kmh) better than the 318tds that it replaced. But the icing on the cake was the potential 49.6mpg – an 11 per cent improvement in fuel economy over the 318tds.

With BMW having made big advances in safety, refinement and equipment levels, the good news continued with the E46 range when it came to running costs. Thanks to the maintenance levels for the new car being considerably lower than the old, they cost rather less to run. The E36 had used a Service Interval Indicator to tell the driver when the next service was due. This was carried over to the E46, but whereas the previous car had typically needed a service every 9,000 miles, the new one stretched that to an average of 14,750 miles. With careful driving it could be eked out even further to 18,500 miles – a figure not to be sniffed at when many cars were still needing to have routine maintenance every 10,000 miles. Such extended service

The second derivative in the E46 range was the Coupé – which was every bit as stylish as its forebear; this is a 323Ci. (BMW)

periods were possible thanks to the adoption of chain-driven camshafts, automatic valve adjustment, a solid state distributor, self-adjusting clutch and stainless steel exhausts along with long-life air filters and spark plugs – among other things.

Of course, all these things added to the initial cost of buying one of the cars, but this was why the 3-Series was a premium small car – and such moves were worthwhile because the typical car would need just four visits to the garage in its first 60,000 miles instead of the previous seven, helping to reduce the maintenance costs for the car by nearly a third. Suddenly the 3-Series didn't seem quite so expensive, although the biggest running cost for any car is the depreciation and in this respect the 3-Series could claim to have one of the strongest possible records.

None of the new cars in the 3-Series line up was fitted with an automatic gearbox as standard, but all except for the 320d were available with this as an option. Standard equipment for all cars was a five-speed manual transmission and 318i buyers who opted for a self-shifting gearbox had four ratios at their disposal. Anyone buying a six-cylinder car had a five-speed gearbox complete with a manual sequential option – otherwise known as Steptronic in BMW parlance.

A new Coupé and a Convertible

By the summer of 1999 BMW had developed a new 3-Series Coupé, and just like its predecessor it was effectively a two-door saloon with a sharply raked rear window. The previous Coupé had accounted for 18 per

cent of 3-Series production, with a not insignificant 470,000 examples rolling off the production lines in six years of production. Just like the E36, the E46 Coupé shared the practicality of its forebear but also oozed style. When Russell Bulgin tried out one of the first test cars he declared the car was 'beyond compare'. But that was partly on account of it really having no real rivals because other car makers were taking a different route to tackling the coupé market, preferring instead to offer a hatch rather than a saloon configuration.

Once again, there was relatively little in common with the four-door saloon – BMW claimed the only parts shared between the saloon and the coupé were the door handles, side repeater lamps and BMW badges. To ensure the proportions were much sportier than the saloon's, the dimensions also differed in every plane. Not only was the Coupé 17mm longer but it was also 18mm wider and 46mm lower. At the same time, the headlamps were slimmer, the tail lamps longer and the windscreen angle more shallow. The exterior was familiar, yet it was so different, while the interior was well-known to anyone who had sat in a saloon.

At first there were no four-cylinder cars available, the line-up being restricted to the 323Ci and 328Ci – the arrival of the Coupé saw the introduction of a new naming convention with Ci denoting a two-door car. But by the end of the year there was also a 318Ci and by the following summer there was an even more stylish two-door 3-Series as the all-new Convertible had made its debut at the 2000 Geneva Motor Show. The new car was to be built in-house at BMW's

Regensburg factory having been developed completely in-house. As with the Coupé, at first only a six-cylinder powerplant was available: a 2.5-litre unit in the 323Ci. Mated to a five-speed manual gearbox there was also a Steptronic transmission available and under the skin everything was pretty much the same as for the Coupé. The main difference between the closed car's construction and the open car's was the amount of stiffening required – while the lack of scuttle shake was impressive, the Convertible was a hefty 224kg (494lb) heavier than its closed equivalent. At 1,669kg (3,680lb) that was a lot of weight to carry around, although some of this was due to the electric hood mechanism. Despite the extra weight, the top speed was just 4mph (6kmh) slower than the 323Ci Coupé, at 137mph (220kmh). The 0–62mph dash could also be despatched in just 8.2 seconds, thanks to a torque figure of 181lb ft, the power output being 170bhp. Regardless of these figures, the car proved itself capable of travelling nearly 34 miles (55km) on a single gallon of unleaded when it was put through its paces by *Autocar* magazine. As well as its frugality the testers also commented on the fact that the superb dynamics of the Coupé hadn't been compromised with the loss of the roof – although the extra weight could make itself felt, unsurprisingly.

Within a couple of months the 323Ci had been joined by the 330Ci Convertible, using the new 3.0-litre engine that replaced the 2.8-litre unit and by September 2000

The Convertible was even more stylish than the Coupé, and looked great whether the hood was raised or stowed. (BMW)

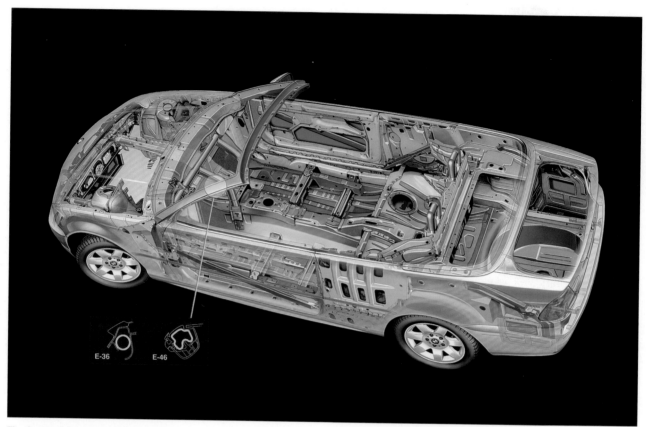

The Convertible was also just as good to drive as the Coupé, thanks to its immensely stiff construction. (BMW)

the 323Ci had been replaced by the 325Ci. This brought with it 24 valves in place of the previous 12 and with the adoption of Double-VANOS technology there was also an increase in power, to 192bhp. Having gradually moved the 3-Series Coupé and Convertible upmarket, a cheaper alternative was introduced in Autumn 2000 –

The two-door versions of the E46 (Coupé and Convertible) were badged as Ci models, to separate them from the more practical saloon and Touring. (BMW)

the 320Ci. Contrary to the car's badging, the new powerplant displaced 2.2 litres, and offered up to 170bhp and 155lb ft from its six cylinders. That was enough to give a top speed of 138mph (222kmh) with a five-speed manual gearbox – although there was the option of a five-speed Steptronic transmission. Alongside the 320Ci, Sport derivatives of the 325Ci and 330Ci were introduced, bringing with them 18in alloy wheels, sports seats, an M steering wheel and M aerodynamic body styling.

A new Touring

BMW had an especially busy year in 1999, because as well as the all-new Coupé and Convertible making their debuts, there was a completely new Touring. The model was still a 'lifetstyle estate', which meant style was higher up the list of priorities than practicality, but BMW had still made an effort to make it much more spacious inside than the E36 Touring had been. There were four petrol engines available from the start: one four-cylinder and three six-cylinder units. These were the 318i, 320i, 325i and 330i, with the oil-burning 330d being added in Spring 2000. In some markets there was also the chance to buy a Touring with the 2.0-litre diesel engine, which used the same 1,951cc four-cylinder engine that had already been seen in the

3-Series saloon. The 50:50 front:rear weight distribution of the saloon was retained but other than the addition of a new bodystyle, in terms of the underpinnings the Touring carried everything over from the saloon.

The final E46 incarnation of the quartet was the Touring. It was the fourth BMW to carry the name, but only the third 3-Series. (BMW)

In common with its predecessor, the E46 Touring put style above practicality, but it was still much more spacious than the model before it. (BMW)

330d

Towards the end of the 1990s there were some astonishingly good diesel engines being produced, especially by European car makers. But there were still many who doubted that an oil-burning engine could ever have the edge over a petrol one. However, anyone who drove the 330d, launched in Summer 2000, was instantly converted. Here was a car which had near-supercar performance (at least in terms of usable performance) but which could potentially return up to 40mpg. Even when driven hard it was unlikely to dip below 30mpg, and with 288lb ft of torque on offer – which equated to 189lb ft per tonne – it was no wonder the car was so rapid. To put that into perspective, the most potent petrol-powered 3-Series at that time was the 328i, and that had to concede 81lb ft to the newcomer, so it was no wonder that with its much more frugal nature, the 330d held so much appeal. Of course, the 330d had a power band that was rather narrower than the 328i's, there was still that familiar diesel rattle at start up and there was also a 125kg

Even the 320d paled into insignificance when the 330d was introduced – six cylinders, huge torque and potentially economy as well. It had it all. (BMW)

(276lb) weight penalty. All that paled into insignificance as soon as the car was moving, although on paper the car's performance didn't look that impressive. A top speed of 141mph (227kmh) and a 0–62mph time of 7.8 seconds was hardly what you would call exceptional, but the reality was that this was the first diesel-powered car that had more performance than most drivers were likely to ever use.

Soon after BMW had introduced the six-cylinder 3-litre diesel engine, it repeated the trick with a petrol-powered equivalent. The 330i superseded the 328i – and was even better. (BMW)

330i arrives

In Spring 2000, a 2,979cc petrol engine replaced the 2.8-litre unit that had topped off the BMW 3-Series range for the previous five years. Although this new 3.0-litre engine was essentially the same unit as the old, it wasn't just given an extra 186cc. As was typical with BMW, although the power and torque levels had been increased, efficiency was improved which meant the emissions figures were reduced. Although the new powerplant was an evolution of the old all-aluminium unit, it was given its own engine number (M54 in place of M52) which illustrated just how far-reaching the changes were.

There were various reasons for the increased efficiency, but the main ones were the introduction of an electronic throttle into the engine management system, the idle speed was lowered, piston friction was reduced and the range of valve timing was also increased. The result was an increase in power of 38bhp but without any penalty in increased fuel consumption. BMW even went so far as to explain how the introduction of a longer stroke – necessitating a new crankshaft – was directly responsible for 11.6bhp of that extra power. Tweaking the Double VANOS system also liberated an extra 4.8bhp but the majority of the extra power (22bhp) was directly attributable to smoothing out the induction and exhaust flows. As well as the increase in power there was an equivalent hike in torque as well. There was 221lb ft on tap from 3,500rpm, but 90 per cent of that (199lb ft) was available from just 1,500rpm – no wonder the car was so driveable!

When the 330i was launched, the E46 M3 was yet to be seen, so the only comparisons that could be made were with the outgoing M3 Evolution. While that car was certainly fast and dynamically superb, it was based on the E36 – so it was no surprise that the 330i, and in particular the 330Ci, could give it a run for its money. As *Car* magazine had done a few years earlier, *Autocar* questioned whether or not there really was any point in buying an M3 when the 330Ci was so capable: 'You seriously begin to wonder who needs an M3's extra performance, especially when the top speeds are identical. For most people the 330Ci's blend of outright performance, driver appeal and real-world refinement is close to perfection.' The reason for these words was the fact that this new slingshot from the BMW stable was capable of despatching the 0–62mph sprint in a mere 6.5 seconds while enjoying the same electronically limited top speed of 155mph (249kmh) – quick enough for any reasonable driver, surely?

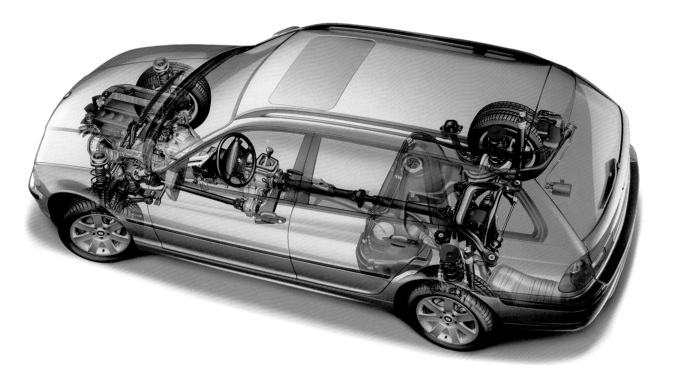

As with the E36, in some markets there was the chance to buy a four-wheel-drive 3-Series, but right-hand drive wasn't available. (BMW)

The key to the 330Ci's huge desirability wasn't just the on-paper performance. While acceleration and top speed tell part of the story, the reason why the car was judged so complete was the even sharper steering, the more able cornering and the more reassuring handling. The flat torque curve that is so important in a car that aims to offer true driveability was very much in evidence and from 2,000rpm the car would pull like a train. In fact, even in fifth, with just 1,200rpm on the clock, the engine just picked up cleanly and projected the car towards the horizon. It was no surprise that comparisons were made with V8 and V12 powerplants, such was the unit's tractability. Although six-speed gearboxes were starting to become fashionable, the 330i made do with a five-speed transmission. Those who preferred to let the gearbox do the ratio changing could specify an automatic transmission and to ensure that the auto wasn't significantly slower than the manual version, the final drive ratio was reduced from 3.07:1 to 3.38:1. Helping to rein in the power there were bigger brakes than before, and larger wheels to house them: 17in seven-spoke wheels were standard for all 330is and the ventilated discs that were fitted all round grew by 26mm, to become 326mm at the front and 320mm at the rear.

Alongside the 330Ci Coupé there were also saloon and Touring versions of the 3.0-litre car available. Like the Coupé, they also benefited from the extended service intervals which were aimed at reducing running costs for those fortunate enough to be able to afford the near-£30,000 car. The four-wheel-drive version, the 330iX, was not offered in the UK as it was only available in left-hand-drive form, for Continental buyers. This was not intended to be a proper off-roader – although you could say the same thing about the X3, which is an off-roader that you wouldn't actually take off road. The real benefit of the four-wheel-drive 330i was that at high speeds on the autobahn the car was much more stable, although the 17mm higher centre of gravity didn't do the car many favours when it came to turning corners.

As was customary with BMW's range-topping six-cylinder cars, nobody could find any serious flaws in the formula, but somehow BMW managed to keep improving things. From March 2001, the 330i Sport saloon was fitted with new aerodynamic front and rear body styling and an M Sports multi-function steering wheel, as well as the 18in alloy wheels, sports seats, sports suspension, Alcantara upholstery and other interior cosmetic features of the existing Sport models. The 325i Sport and 330d Sport followed later in the spring. Alongside these cars, the Sport Touring models offered the same equipment and engines as the saloon, starting with the 330i in March and followed later by the 325i and 330d.

325i and 330i SMG

The E36 M3 had introduced the concept of a sequential manual gearbox (SMG) and the E46 M3 had built on that with a system which was much better. So when an SMG II system became available on the 325i and 330i in Autumn 2001, BMW's customers were waiting expectantly. By the time the new generation of SMG had been developed for the E46 M3, it was receiving great acclaim – and the 330i was surely deserving of such a great transmission. Well, yes it was, but the regular E46 didn't get the same SMG set-up that was fitted to the M car, as Magnetti Marelli made the former unit and Siemens made the latter. Also, the M3's gearbox was equipped with six ratios whereas its lesser siblings had just five. Something both versions had in common though, was the fitment of just two pedals, and although it was possible to stick to changing gears manually, there was also the option of a fully automatic mode.

Although the technology between the two varieties of SMG was quite different, it was used in much the same way. This meant there were paddle shifts behind the

The six-cylinder 3-Series Coupés were available with BMW's SMG II transmission from Autumn 2001 – and it was far better than the earlier system as first seen on the E36 M3. (BMW)

steering wheel and these operated a high-pressure hydraulic shift mechanism, but in keeping with its lower specification, the new SMG system featured just four modes, compared with the M3's 11. These were 'normal', 'cruise', 'sport' and 'launch', the latter being offered to give the best possible sprint time. By selecting launch mode it was possible to match the manual-gearbox 330i's 0–62mph time of 6.5 seconds, with the clutch being dropped once engine revs had reached 4,000rpm, and the change from first to second gear taking just 150 milliseconds. Normal gearchange times were more like 450 milliseconds, but if sport mode was chosen this would be closer to 250 milliseconds – anyone who could change gear in the manual gearbox car in a quarter of a second was doing well!

E46 facelift

By October 2001 it was time for the E46 to have a facelift, although BMW preferred to use the term 'new car', on account of there being two new four-cylinder engines, extensive chassis changes, improved standard specifications and, for the saloon and Touring models, amended styling. The reason only these models were changed is because the Compact and 330i/Ci models had incorporated these amendments since they were

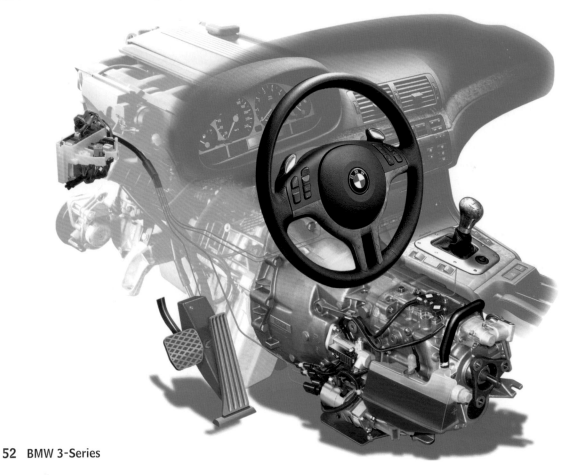

launched in April 2001. New, curved headlights, incorporating the indicators behind clear glass, and round fog lamps were joined by a wider kidney grille which led into a newly styled bonnet 'powerdome' which ran up to the A-pillars. There was also a new swage line on the front wings, with a teardrop-shaped repeater indicator along with a new front air dam, new rear valance and – on the saloon – revised rear light clusters. Under the skin there were also changes – changes which BMW felt were innovative enough to be called revolutionary. Along with the new engines there was a new sequential sports gearbox (SSG) and extensive suspension and steering changes to improve the agility of the 3-Series.

The first of the new four-cylinder engines was fitted to the 318i; a Valvetronic 16-valve 2-litre unit. This meant that the new 318i was only the second car to be fitted with Valvetronic technology, the first being the E46 316Ti Compact, which had been launched in Summer 2001. The Valvetronic technology removed the need for a throttle butterfly, controlling valve lift infinitely to control the fuel/air mixture supply. The benefit was an engine which produced 21.2 per cent more power than its predecessor, and 11.1 per cent more torque, but which still managed an 11 per cent improvement in fuel economy with a consequent reduction in carbon dioxide emissions. This meant the new car produced 143bhp at 6,000rpm, 25bhp more

than its predecessor. Allied to that was a torque increase of 14lb ft at 3,750 rpm, with a resulting top speed of 135mph (217kmh) and 0–62mph acceleration time of 9.3 seconds.

It wasn't just the four-cylinder petrol engine that received the engineers' attention, as the 16-valve four-cylinder diesel unit in the 320d was also heavily revised. Available in the saloon, Touring and Compact, this new oil burner delivered 10 per cent more power, 17.9 per cent more torque and a fuel consumption improvement of 3.6 per cent over its predecessor. With 150bhp (the same as the 2.0-litre six-cylinder petrol engine of 1998) and 243lb ft of torque, the 320d was able to despatch the 0–62mph sprint in 8.9 seconds while also achieving a top speed of 134mph (216kmh) – although the ability to dismiss 50–75mph (80–121kmh) in fifth gear in just 7.5 seconds was a neat trick which its competitors struggled to match.

It was no surprise that with the advent of models like the 320d, sales of diesel cars were increasing across Europe. Combined with the impressive performance figures were fuel consumption figures which a petrol engine would never be able to match. The official figures claimed by BMW for the 320d were an average

The E46 was facelifted in 2002, when it was given a sharper nose. This coincided with the launch of the first 316i Touring, with a 1.9-litre engine. (BMW)

The saloon, Convertible and Coupé all received a restyled nose, with different headlamps, for the 2003 model year. New rear lamps were also fitted. (BMW)

of 51.4mpg, while extra-urban cruising allowed up to 64.2mpg. With its 13.9-gallon tank, that meant a range of up to 893 miles (1,437km) – although of course, few drivers (if any) would ever be able to achieve such economy in the real world.

The secret of the 320d's performance lay in the second-generation high-pressure common rail fuel injection system, which operated at 1600 bar – a first for a large-scale production diesel engine. Together with a volume-controlled fuel pump, a new digital diesel electronic engine management system, twin balance shafts and an improved variable-valve turbocharger, BMW felt justified in claiming this was a new engine. To go with these powerplants there was a choice of three transmissions. All 318i and 320d models were fitted as standard with five-speed manual gearboxes which as an option – and for the first time on BMW's four-cylinder diesel – a five-speed automatic transmission with adaptive learning and Steptronic was made available. For the 325i and 330i saloon and Coupé models, BMW continued to offer a sequential sports gearbox.

SSG was an automated manual gearbox with its gears selected in a sequential pattern, like those on a motorcycle. The product of Formula 1 technology, it

enabled the driver to select gears with a flick of the gear lever, via paddles behind the steering wheel, or simply by letting the gearbox select the gears itself in automatic mode. SSG also offered various modes depending on how and where the car was being driven. 'C', or 'Cruise' mode, was an automated programme for a city environment. A 'Sport' button behind the gear lever activated faster, more sporting gear changes and offered a 'launch control' programme to enable perfect 0–60mph times.

To make the most of these engine and transmission refinements, the chassis of the 3-Series also received some tweaks to make it sharper. Among the changes were completely revised settings for the springs and dampers along with stiffer rubber mountings for the suspension. To go with these there was a faster, more direct steering rack that required only three turns from lock to lock.

In April 2002, the new 316i saloon arrived, to replace the previous 316i which had been taken out of production in Summer 2001. As this was traditionally BMW's second best seller after the 318i saloon, the model's success was critical to the company. Powered by the M42 1.8-litre Valvetronic engine, the new 316i offered more power and torque, better acceleration and a higher top speed than its predecessor. But yet again, despite these performance improvements, fuel consumption for the new car was reduced by 11 per cent with the attendant benefit of lower CO_2 emissions

of 172 grams/km. Perhaps of more interest was the fact that the introduction of this new, 1.8-litre 316i also saw the arrival of the first 316i Touring. Even with the new engine, the revs had to be used if the car was fully laden, so it was no surprise that BMW hadn't offered a 316i Touring before, with even less power on tap. But even if the power levels weren't that high, the rest of the chassis was every bit as good as the rest of the Touring range, so it was a delight to drive whether or not there were huge amounts of power in reserve.

330Ci Clubsport

Having paid attention to the bottom of the 3-Series range with the introduction of the new 316i, in May 2002 the 330Ci Clubsport Coupé arrived, powered by the standard 231bhp 3.0-litre straight-six engine. It sat between the 330Ci Sport and the M3 Coupé and was distinguished by its new rear M spoiler and a new design of 18in double-spoke alloy wheels. There were also sports suspension settings and 20kg (44lb) of insulation material was removed to increase engine noise in the cabin. Inside there were leather and Alcantara sports seats, a shortened M gear lever, the door sills featured the Clubsport model designation and silver aluminium cubed interior trim was fitted as standard. Just three colours were offered: Titanium Silver, Estoril Blue and Velvet blue. So far so good, but it carried a hefty price premium compared with the standard 330Ci yet it was no better to drive – not that

Seen by most as a cynical way of charging more while giving less, the 330Ci Clubsport looked great but offered little extra over the standard car. (BMW)

that was such a bad thing, as the standard car was so good. The verdict of most who tried it reckoned the Clubsport was merely a cynical marketing exercise, which looked less polished than the car on which it was based – yet it cost significantly more, offered no more performance and still didn't come equipped with a CD player as standard. No wonder people chose the standard car in preference to the not-so-special 'special' version.

330Cd

In Spring 2003, BMW introduced its first diesel-powered coupé; the 330Cd. A new version of BMW's highly acclaimed 3.0-litre straight-six oil-burner was fitted so the company was hardly taking a gamble on the car

DID YOU KNOW?

The E46 pioneered the use of the contact-free brake light switch, which meant that the unit would never wear out as it relied purely on electronic signals for its operation. In an attempt to introduce other components that would work for the life of the car, BMW also fitted LEDs instead of bulbs to the instrument cluster on the dash.

By mixing a fabulous bodyshell and chassis with the world's best
diesel engine, BMW could do no wrong with the launch of the
3-litre 330Cd. (BMW)

being accepted. After all, this engine and the
3-Series were universally liked, so by combining the two
the end result was always going to be highly regarded.
With Mercedes having introduced its diesel CLK coupé
and Audi its diesel-powered cabriolet, BMW simply had
to produce something with which to compete in this
market sector. This engine had always been well-liked,
but for the 330Cd the new unit was even better than the
old with the power output up to 204bhp and torque
improved to 302lb ft, but it was the increase in low
down torque that made the engine so special. The peak
was available from just 1,500rpm, making the in-gear
times quite exceptional. The top speed of 150mph
(241kmh) was also pretty special, as was the 0–62mph
time of 7.2 seconds, but the killer punch was the
economy, which could be as much as 42.8mpg on the
combined cycle. No petrol engine could deliver such
urge to match this. Of course, if the performance

potential was used to the full there was no way the car
would deliver such impressive fuel consumption figures,
but at least the potential was there – helped in no small
part by the six-speed manual gearbox. Unlike the unit
seen before in the 3-Series, top gear was not an
overdrive ratio – maximum speed was achieved in sixth
with five closely space ratios along the way.

The introduction of the 330Cd coincided with the
arrival of a facelifted 3-Series coupé, although the
changes were not especially great. New rear light
clusters incorporated LEDs in place of the bulbs
previously fitted and slightly modified headlamp units
were joined by a new rear air dam, a more pronounced
bonnet bulge and a different style of 17in alloy wheels.
The revised rear light clusters filtered through to the
convertible 3-Series at the same time – and they were
more complicated than it first appeared. The brake
lighting was a two-stage system which illuminated
more intensely if the driver was braking hard. Not only
that, but because LEDs light up much faster than a
conventional bulb, drivers behind would get earlier
warning of the car braking. While they were at it BMW

The final piece in the E46 jigsaw was the X3, launched at the 2003 Frankfurt Motor Show. (BMW)

also began to offer the SMG transmission on the 325Ci and range-topping 330Ci convertible. Buyers of the 330Ci who didn't want this gearbox could have a six-speed manual transmission and those who bought a 3-Series Coupé or Convertible from the facelifted line up got some rather neat adaptive headlights which turned with the front wheels to light the car's way. BMW claimed the technology was revolutionary, but Citroën had been doing the same thing in the 1970s – although of course the system was nothing like as complex, as the light units themselves weren't bi-xenon and there were no computers involved.

The X3

The final instalment in the E46 story was unveiled officially just as this book was going to press. It was the X3, shown for the first time at the September 2003 Frankfurt Motor Show. Building on the huge success of its bigger brother the X5, the smaller off-roader was aimed directly at the Land Rover Freelander, although BMW's car was rather more expensive. The xActivity, covered separately in Chapter Seven, had given a

pretty good idea of what the X3 would look like, and it didn't disappoint. The black bumpers and cladding were a bit of a surprise as it made the car look more downmarket than it was, but colour-coded items are bound to appear in time. The 'flame-surfacing' that Chris Bangle had introduced to the BMW range was in evidence, but toned down so that the car wasn't shunned.

BMW paid close attention to lowering the centre of gravity as much as possible, its ride height being nearly 100mm lower than the Freelander's. With a permanent four-wheel-drive system (dubbed xDrive) fitted as standard to all models, the car's dynamics were up to the usual standards expected of BMW. At launch, there were three six-cylinder engines available – the 2.5-litre and 3.0-litre petrol units alongside the 3.0-litre diesel. These were all offered with a six-speed manual gearbox as standard with the option of a five-speed Steptronic.

Chapter **Four**

The M3

There can be few motoring brands that are more powerful than BMW's M-Sport, thanks to the all-conquering M3 and M5. Backed up by a strong motorsport pedigree, the M badge isn't just marketing puff – it's a genuine case of developing new technologies for the racetrack which are then incorporated into road cars. BMW set up its BMW Motorsport GmbH subsidiary in 1972, to ensure that the company fared as well as possible in motorsport – more than 30 years later the division has become known simply as BMW M. One of the first things the division did (in terms of road car development) was to design and build a concept called the Turbo. With gullwing doors and a mid-mounted 2002 Turbo engine, the Turbo was nothing more than a showcase for the division's capabilities.

Although the M5 was well established by the time the E46 went on sale, the M brand was still most closely associated with the first-generation M3. (BMW)

There was no intention of putting the car into production, but in 1977 BMW decided to investigate the opportunity of doing just that. Codenamed E26, the car progressed all the way to production and became known as the M1 in the process. That tag marked the introduction of Motorsport's first complete car and the new arrival was fitted with a 3,453cc straight-six which generated 277bhp. A five-speed gearbox was fitted and this car formed the basis for an assault on Group Four racing – in which trim the car was producing close to 450bhp.

When BMW decided to turn its back on Formula 1 at the end of the 1987 season, the company didn't abandon motorsport altogether. Instead, it turned to touring car racing, for which the E30 M3 was developed – a car which attained iconic status almost immediately. Using a highly tuned four-cylinder powerplant, the first M3s were raw, hard-edged sportscars that put driving dynamics above just about everything else. The M3 had been announced in 1985, and although the M635CSi 3.5-litre straight-six used in the M1 and later the M5, was a superb unit, the amount of power it produced was beyond the requirements of the racing cars. The extra weight would also upset the handling balance, so the decision was taken to take the four-cylinder route. After all, even in road trim there was 200bhp on tap – enough to propel the car from a standing start to 60mph in 7.1 seconds and on to a top speed of 139mph (224kmh).

The E30 M3 was always meant to be a no-compromise sports car, and as a result it shared relatively little with the cooking versions of the 3-Series. Apart from the bonnet, none of the major panelwork was carried over and much of the running gear was either bespoke or altered. During the car's relatively short existence, even more hardcore versions were released, namely the Evolutions I, II and III. These

were even more focused driver's cars, with generally sharper handling, less weight and more power with each progression. Perhaps the only derivative released which caused doubts about BMW's commitment to the M3 brand was the convertible, which was necessarily seen as something that was more for show than go by the very nature of its far less stiff bodyshell. After all, by choppping off the roof, handling had to be adversely affected, making this the first of the E30 M3s which did not put ultimate handling at the top of the priority list.

The E36 M3

By the time the E36 M3 was released for sale, the car had become far more civilised than many expected. Because the E30 M3 had proved to be so popular, it was entirely predictable that there would be a performance version of the new car. But buyers had to wait before it made its first appearance, as the E30 M3 didn't go out of production until Summer 1991, when the final M3 convertible was produced. It was then more than a year before the E36 M3 was even shown, making its debut at the October 1992 Paris Motor Show. At first the M3 was available only with two-door coupé bodywork, which is one of the reasons why it made its debut rather later than the first derivatives of the E36 range. BMW also wanted to maximise the impact of the car's launch, and

The E30 M3 was a legend in its own lifetime – not to cash in on its iconic status when the E36 was launched would have been a massive wasted opportunity for BMW. (BMW)

by allowing sales of the saloon to settle down, the M3 could be announced with much fanfare. Where the E30 M3 had exuded typical 1980s brashness, the new car was understated in the extreme. In fact many felt it was too understated as it didn't stand far enough apart from the standard 3-Series Coupé. But things had changed since the E30 had gone on sale and discretion was by now preferable to flaunting such available performance.

Instead of a highly tuned four-cylinder engine there was a smoother, much more relaxed six-pot under the bonnet. Driving it was consequently less frenetic and many were dismayed that the car had become more of a boulevard cruiser, but the car's appeal would have

DID YOU KNOW?

BMW built a prototype E30 M3 Touring, marrying practicality with outrageously strong performance. The car was tested at 150mph (241kmh) but with already strong demand for the saloon, coupé and convertible versions of the M3, BMW decided there was no need to expand the range any further.

BMW's Motorsport division

BMW Motorsport GmbH was officially formed on 1 May 1972. There were initially 35 employees and the head of the group was Jochen Neerpasch, an ex-Porsche works driver who had become Ford's racing manager before moving to BMW. Among the drivers he hired were Chris Amon, Hans-Joachim Stuck and Dieter Quester – men who would be responsible for the honing of the division's cars and in whose hands the Motorsport reputation would be built. The first

The M1 was the first car to be produced entirely by BMW Motorsport – the division's usual role was to develop BMW's existing models. (BMW)

cars Motorsport worked on were a 2.0-litre 16-valve 2002, and the fabled 3.0 CSL. The 2002's weight was pared down to 950kg (2,095lb) and with a 240bhp four-cylinder engine under the bonnet there was no shortage of go. But it was the CSL which became a true landmark car, with its 3.0-litre six-cylinder engine and lightweight aluminium panels on a steel monocoque. With 360bhp and a weight of just 1,092kg (2,408lb) the car became the most successful touring car of its day. Chris Amon won the Nürburgring Touring Car Grand Prix at the first attempt, Niki Lauda won the championship race at Monza and the Le Mans Touring Car category was BMW's.

To go with the new venture a distinctive colour scheme was introduced, which was a white background with three stripes along

it – blue, violet and red. This featured on those first racing cars and it became BMW M's trademark. The colour scheme was used on the 3.0 CSL throughout the 1970s and between 1973 and 1979 the car won the European Championship no fewer than six times. That in itself is an impressive track record, but the fact that it featured BMW's first ever four-valve six-cylinder engine makes it all the more remarkable. Although BMW did not compete directly in Formula 2, 50 of its 2.0-litre 16-valve engines were sold to March. Once again, there was tremendous success as a result – out of 16 races the cars won no fewer than 11. By 1975, the focus had shifted to the USA, where the IMSA series was contested, and as a result, market awareness of the BMW brand increased massively over there.

Initially, Motorsport GmbH had a brief to build racing cars only, but their success on the track meant more and more buyers wanted to buy into the brand with cars they could drive on the road. This led to the introduction of versions of the 530, 533i and 535i which had been tweaked by Motorsport. By 1980, no fewer than 895 examples of the 5-Series had been prepared by Motorsport, with various changes made to the engines, brakes and suspension. A turning point came in 1978 when the M1 was introduced, as this was a car produced by Motorsport GmbH, but it wasn't based on a production saloon. Although it was developed first and foremost as a competition car, because the homologation rules decreed that 400 roadgoing cars also had to be built, there was a more civilised version engineered for production. Even though the price was set at DM100,000, demand still exceeded supply. This was no doubt helped by the M1 being the fastest road-going production car built in Germany at the time, with a top speed of 164mph (264kmh) achieved by one magazine test.

Spurred on by the success of the M1, the next project for Motorsport GmbH was a 5-Series that carried M badges. Using the 12-valve six-cylinder engine from the 735i, the M535i was introduced in 1980 and straight away it received rave reviews. Aside from the M1 it was Motorsport's (and hence BMW's) fastest car, with a top speed of around 140mph (225kmh) possible thanks to the 218bhp powerplant. Yet it looked no more sporting than a basic 518, unless the optional front air dam and rear spoiler were specified – here was the ultimate Q-car. When *Car* magazine tested one of the first cars, the only criticisms it could make was inadequate ventilation, along with a bit too much wind noise. It was considered that the balance of superb brakes, fine handling, near-supercar performance and smoothness combined with comfort were enough to make the car well worth the money.

In 1980, Motorsport's focus turned to Formula One. BMW had decided to compete in the formula, which would enable the company to showcase its four-cylinder 1.5-litre engine. This was essentially the same powerplant that was to be found in BMW's production cars, and with a turbocharger and much attention to detail it was possible to extract a reliable 800bhp. Perhaps more

significantly, the engine featured digital motor electronics to keep everything in check – the first time this had been done in Formula One and something which would filter through into the road cars. Brabham entered its first Formula One race using the new BMW engine in 1982 and, by the end of the following season, the World Championship belonged to Brabham BMW.

By 1983, there were 380 people working at Motorsport GmbH and the division was made officially responsible for the development of high-performance road cars as well as masterminding BMW's motorsport programme. In addition to engineering ever-more sophisticated engines, Motorsport's remit included creating better suspension and steering systems. The result of this was the introduction of the M5 and M635CSi in 1984, both of which used the 286bhp straight-six of the M1. Once again, the M5 looked pretty tame – yet could manage 152mph (245kmh) – while the 635CSi only looked fast because of its sports coupé lines; other than that it was pretty understated. Until this point there had been no shortage of projects which had created, maintained and even boosted Motorsport's reputation.

In 1986, the biggest project that the subsidiary had ever worked on came to fruition – the E30 M3. Not only was this to be the most successful Touring Car ever, but it also became BMW's biggest selling Motorsport road car. As the M3 was to compete in Group A racing, at least 5,000 road cars had to be produced and because the projects that Motorsport was working on were getting larger all the time, the decision was made to relocate the division. From its inception, the home of Motorsport had always been at Preussenstrasse near Munich, but in 1986, it was relocated to Garching, also near Munich. Once installed there, development of the M3 continued apace and by the end of production, no fewer than 17,100 E30 M3s had been produced, including over 1,400 convertibles.

By the time the second-generation M5 was introduced in 1986, it was taken for granted that there would be a Motorsport version. There was even a Touring version as well, although it wasn't available at first, and just 650 were built. Using a 3.6-litre engine, the first of these M5s offered 315bhp and nearly 160mph (257kmh) – but when the capacity was increased to 3.8 litres, power consequently rose to 340bhp and the top speed to nearer 170mph (274kmh). A decade earlier those figures would have looked pretty good for most supercars, but in a family saloon capable of seating five in comfort, they were nothing short of astonishing. This car paved the way for a softer, less frenetic M3 when the E30 gave way to the E36, the evolution of which is covered in the main text, along with the introduction of the M Roadster and M Coupé.

In 2002, the Motorsport division turned out 27,000 cars, 24,000 of which were examples of the M3. As well as 2,400 M5s there were 700 M Coupés and Roadsters. The group has certainly come a long way since its inception in May 1972.

The E36 M3 was much less hard-core than its predecessor, and it was initially available as a coupé only. (BMW)

been necessarily limited by making it too much of a driver's car. Despite this change of focus for the M3, whoever tested the car eulogised over its performance, handling, build quality and comfort. Although the engine now featured six cylinders, it was still developed by BMW's Motorsport division. That gave BMW the best of both worlds, as buyers expected six cylinders – after all, that was what BMW had become famed for – but they also expected something a bit special in terms of powerplant development. By allowing the Motorsport

The E36 introduced BMW's variable-valve timing VANOS system, which was to become Double-VANOS when the M3 Evo was launched. (BMW)

boys to work their magic it was clear that the engine's potential had been maximised.

The basis of the Motorsport division's attentions was the M50 engine, in 2,990cc form. This capacity had been arrived at by increasing both the bore and stroke of the standard unit, so that the dimensions were now 86mm and 85.8mm respectively and the result was a power output of 286bhp at 7,000rpm with a torque figure of 231lb ft at 3,600rpm. While it is obvious that such a power output isn't to be dismissed, what is much more impressive is that the engine featured the highest specific output of any normally aspirated car available anywhere in the world. With 96bhp per litre on tap, there was no other engine that could boast such efficiency.

It wasn't just the increase in displacement which had led to such outputs – the engine management system was also reprogrammed to optimise the fuelling and ignition – but the big development was the variable valve timing system introduced on the M3. With 16 valves and a pair of overhead camshafts already standard on the M50 engine, the best way of improving the breathing was by improving the air flow at high revs but without sacrificing low-end torque – something which could only be done by using valve timing which altered as the engine revs increased. Carrying the VANOS name, this innovation produced an incredibly flat torque curve and in time the technology found its way into all of BMW's petrol engines.

Having made such a leap forward with the engine, it would have made little sense for corners to be cut with the rest of the running gear. Whereas the E30 M3 had used a gearbox incorporating a dog-leg first gear, the E36 version used the same conventional unit found in other E36 cars – or at least those equipped with the five-speed manual transmission. Anyone wanting a self-shifting gearbox in an M3 was disappointed, as BMW decided that such a move would have been a compromise too far, and no true racing car for the road would have an automatic transmission. The five closely spaced ratios were finished off with a direct-drive top gear, rather than incorporating an overdrive and there was a 25 per cent limited slip differential to ensure the power could be put down as effectively as possible. It was thanks to such closely spaced ratios and the increased rev limit that the car was able to post incredibly quick acceleration times.

The 3-Series was already such a sporting car that the M3 started out with an excellent base on which to build. This meant the basic suspension architecture could be retained, although it was developed significantly to distance it from the common-or-garden models. The front and rear anti-roll bars were strengthened and components such as the wheelbearings and stub axles were strengthened to cope with the higher cornering forces likely to be generated. Progressive-rate dampers were also fitted, which were around 10 per cent stiffer than those normally specified for an M Technic-tweaked E36 coupé. As befitting a car with such monstrous performance, the braking system was beefed up significantly to cope with the repeated stops from high speeds that the car was likely to have to cope with. Naturally, the system consisted of ventilated discs front and rear, the diameter of which was uprated over those of the standard E36 resulting in the front discs being a whopping 315mm in diameter at the front, and 313mm at the back. To house such huge brakes, 17in 10-spoke alloy wheels were fitted, complete with low-profile (235/40 ZR 17) tyres. The wheels fitted as standard had a width of 7.5in, but if that wasn't enough it was possible to opt for wheels at the back which were an inch wider.

The 3-Series had always been famed for its superb cabin, so relatively little needed to be done to the M3's interior to make it worthy of a range-topper. More supportive seats were fitted with suede edging and the instrumentation was changed slightly – M3 owners were unlikely to be too concerned with what BMW's famous econometer had to say, so an oil temperature gauge was fitted in its place. Perhaps more in keeping with the Motorsport ethos was not how much

Although the M3 was recognisably different from its Coupé siblings, it was still very understated despite its huge capabilities. (LAT)

equipment could be shoehorned into the cabin, but rather how much weight could be shed to maximise the car's performance. After all, BMW had paid great attention to detail to squeeze even more power out of the M50 engine so to make the most of this extra grunt it also had to reduce the car's weight as far as possible without compromising its refinement. Even the rear window glass was thinner to make the car a few kilos lighter.

Not surprisingly, those who drove the car eulogised over its impressive performance, predictable handling and peerless build quality. Some also disliked its understated looks, but for most that was another of the car's many strong points – most people buying the M3 would be doing so because it didn't shout about the potential that was there waiting to be unleashed. And if they did want something that was less of a Q-car, they could always enlist the help of one of the many aftermarket tuning companies that had sprung up to cater for such owners.

M3 saloon and Convertible

Initially, the M3 was available as a coupé only, but from Spring 1994 a drophead version was offered. The E30 M3 had been available as a Convertible and it was entirely predictable that the E36 would also be offered with a folding roof. Although the car was 80kg (176lb) heavier than its Coupé sibling, and also less aerodynamic, it still managed to sprint from a standing start to 60mph (96kmh) in just 5.7 seconds – the closed car could cut 0.3 seconds from that. Like the Coupé, the Convertible could manage to hit an artificially limited 155mph (250kmh) – indeed, Motorsport managing

There had already been an M3 Convertible derivative of the E30 – its successor was much softer with its six-cylinder engine. (BMW)

director Karl-Heinz Kalbfell reckoned the car would be able to top 175mph (281kmh) without such a restrictor. But this car wasn't so much about performance as the opportunity for BMW to offer a highly specified range topper for the 3-Series line up. Part of the reason for the extra weight was a power-operated hood – something which was available on most other 3-Series at that time. Similarly, the 8.5-inch wide rear wheels which were optional on the M3 Coupé were standard

The M3 saloon was largely unloved, with buyers preferring instead to buy the Coupé or Convertible. (LAT)

on the Convertible while nappa leather trim was also included in the car's £37,500 price.

The third and final body style for the M3 arrived in Summer 1995, when the M3 saloon was introduced. To the extent that this topped off the saloon range in the same way that the M3 Convertible topped off the drophead range, so consequently the equipment levels were high, just like the price. The M3 saloon had come about because of the M5's success – BMW couldn't make enough of this hugely capable autobahnstormer and by introducing a 3-Series in the same vein, buyers could more easily afford this smaller, but still incredibly able saloon. As with most of its cars, BMW opted for the understated look. There were no wild bodykits or ego-boosting add-ons, simply discreet spoilers and equally understated five-spoke alloy wheels.

Although the Coupé and Convertible shared the same style of five-spoke alloys, the saloon had a different, less aggressive set of wheels which were still 17in in diameter and 7.5in wide at the front, with the rears an inch wider. Such monster wheels had to be fitted to house the braking system. The suspension was slightly softer to increase the comfort factor but the car was virtually as fast as its Coupé brother, giving away just one tenth of a second in the 0–60mph sprint. The top speed was the same as the Coupé and Convertible at 155mph thanks to the fitment of an electronic speed limiter that was identical to those fitted to all M3s and because of a weight increase of 15kg (33lb) over its two-door counterpart, the saloon was also slightly slower in covering the standing quarter-mile – 14.3 seconds compared with 13.9 seconds for the Coupé.

M3 Evolution

In Autumn 1995, the European-spec E36 M3 was developed further to become the M3 Evolution. As with the standard car, only the two-door Coupé was available at first but in early 1996 it was joined by the Convertible and saloon, although for the UK market all three were introduced at the same time, in February 1996. Predictably, the Evolution cars featured a more powerful engine, more aggressive styling and equipment changes over the standard cars. To increase the power output from the in-line six, both the bore and stroke were increased to give a capacity of 3,201cc. This was combined with double VANOS, where the variable valve timing was used for the inlet and exhaust valves, whereas the standard car had used variable valve timing for the inlet valves only. All this led to a jump in power to 321bhp at 7,400rpm, which was only possible thanks to a raised red-line – the previous car had been red-lined at 7,250rpm. Torque was also increased, with 258lb ft available at 3,250rpm. The engine changes didn't stop there – to eke as much power as possible from the straight-six a lot more tricks were used including a remapped engine management system (badged MSS50), larger inlet valves, lightweight pistons and graphite-coated con-rods to reduce friction. Despite the substantial increase in power, fuel consumption was reduced thanks to the more efficient engine management, which was developed by BMW in conjunction with Siemens. This greater efficiency meant

that although the top speed was still restricted electronically to 155mph, the car could blitz from a standing start to 62mph in just 5.5 seconds.

To maximise the performance potential of the new engine, something a bit special in the transmission department had to be conjured up. Whereas the old car had used a five-speed manual gearbox, the Evolution had a six-speed manual gearbox derived from the M5's unit. This had five closely spaced ratios for strong acceleration but a high sixth gear for relaxed cruising at high speed. This led to reduced fuel consumption as well as improved refinement, and was also a useful marketing tool – BMW needed to stay ahead of the pack and the company began using six-speed gearboxes before most other car makers. To help put the power down there was a 25 per cent limited slip differential fitted and to help rein in the power a much-improved braking system was installed. Incorporating a new ABS system, this all-disc set-up was derived from the M3 race cars and featured fully floating calipers. To top off the mechanical changes the suspension was revised with new springs and dampers and the steering was sharpened up with a slightly quicker steering rack.

Increasing the power was only part of the process of making the car even sharper with a decrease in weight also playing its part. To that end, on Convertible and Coupé versions of the M3 Evolution, aluminium doors were used instead of steel, which resulted in 12kg (26lb) being shed on each side. Unfortunately, this

The M3 Evolution Coupé arrived in 1995, which was even better than the standard M3 that had first been seen three years earlier. The Convertible arrived a few months later. (BMW)

The M3 Evo was very good, but some questioned whether it was worth a large premium over its smaller brother the 328i.

weight loss was offset by that of increased equipment levels and so the car's kerb weight of 1,440kg (3,175lb) was not that much less than the standard car's 1,520kg (3,352lb). But there was an extra 35bhp to ensure the power-to-weight ratio was a strong, 211bhp/tonne. Extra equipment fitted to the car included integral head restraints in the seats, clear indicator lenses, a matt black grille in the front air dam and leather trim as standard.

It seemed that BMW could do no wrong with its 3-Series or its M brand – mixing the two seemed to be a sure-fire winner. Yet when *Car* magazine tested the M3 Evo against 'its deadliest rival' in 1995, the car seemed to have potentially met its match. And when that rival was from BMW's own stable it was even more worrying, because the 328i was around two-thirds of the price and in the real world, not that much less capable.

Meanwhile, a US-only M3 Evolution was launched,

with a 3,152cc version of the in-line six-cylinder engine. The reduced capacity was because of a shorter stroke and the result was a rather less spectacular increase over the standard car's power output, with 243bhp generated. This was achieved at 6,000rpm while the maximum torque of 236lb ft was available from 3,800rpm. But perhaps the most disappointing aspect of the car – after its relatively lacklustre engine – was the lack of adoption of the six-speed gearbox. Instead, the more usual five-speed item was retained, which was rather surprising considering the extra ratio could have helped with emissions reduction – something federal authorities were becoming increasingly keen to reduce by the time the car went on sale. This focus on emissions was one of the reasons for the use of the slightly smaller engine. California's corporate average fuel economy (CAFE) regulations favoured frugality over power so BMW felt it was justified to turn down the wick a little bit – after all, the US-spec M3 was hardly lacking when compared with both its rivals and BMW's more usual 3-Series models.

There had been a US-only version of the E36 M3 – BMW followed that up with a US-only derivative of the E46 model. (BMW)

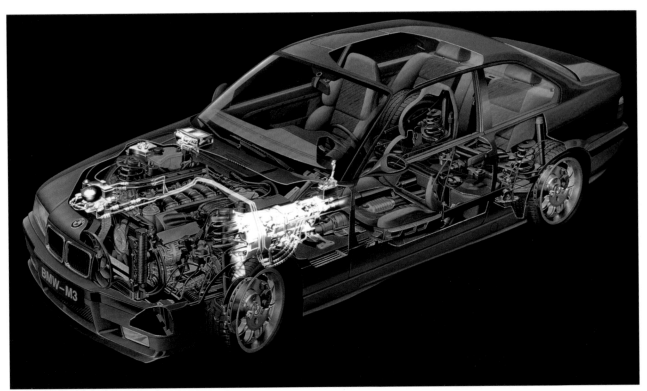

The first sequential manual gearbox went on sale in 1997, and was specified in most M3s sold by BMW. (BMW)

The lack of a six-speed gearbox for the US market paled into insignificance in September 1996, when BMW announced its SMG transmission. Cars equipped with this transmission weren't available in the UK until March 1998, while the first examples had been sold in Europe a year earlier. SMG (sequential manual gearbox) allowed gearchanges in just 150 milliseconds thanks to the clutch pedal being taken care of automatically. Having just two pedals to take care of was one obvious benefit, but another was that with the SMG transmission the gears could be changed with the use of paddle shifts behind the steering wheel or by flicking the gearlever backwards or forwards to go up or down across the six ratios. The transmission could work so quickly because there were no mechanical linkages – instead, everything was controlled by wire, with electronics running the whole system. The gearbox gave the option of fully automatic ratio changes or sequential manual ones, and as soon as it was released the motoring press reviewed it enthusiastically, although there were some reservations about the software being used. The bottom line was that the car could lap the Nürburgring five seconds faster than the standard car, but it wasn't as involving and it was also less controllable – but it was a good first effort.

The introduction of the SMG transmission in September was part of a minor facelift for the whole 3-Series range, the main change for the M3 cars being the adoption of a new M Sport air bag-equipped steering wheel. Exactly a year later the final developments were made before the E36 M3 was superseded by the E46 model. The biggest change for the series was the aluminium doorskins being replaced

The interior of the M3 Evo was much the same as its forebear's – which meant high equipment levels, supportive seats and peerless build quality. (BMW)

The final E36 M3 saloon was handed over to the Bavarian police as a patrol car – being on traffic duties must have never been so attractive! (BMW)

by more conventional steel ones. On 12 December 1997, the 50,000th M3 was built, this also being the last saloon. To commemorate the significance of the car it was handed over to the Bavarian police force to be used as a traffic patrol car. When the final M3 Evo was produced in Spring 1999, there were many who mourned the M3's passing. But the fact that it died only to make way for a newer, better model was cause for celebration indeed, and when that new car arrived, there was even more cause for celebration.

The E46 M3

The M3 brand was 14 years old when the third-generation car arrived. Expectations were high, as by the time the last of the E36 M3s had rolled off the line, the car was still crushingly capable, even though the model on which it was based was around a decade old. The E46, from which the new car was developed was already two years old, but that had given the Motorsport team more time to hone the car's chassis to perfection. When it was first shown in Autumn 2000, reactions had reached fever pitch with every motoring magazine proclaiming in large headlines that this was the car that would beat all comers when it came to driving enjoyment. That was before anybody had even driven the thing – its aggressive stance, superb interior and enticing on-paper specifications suggesting that once the car was put through its paces all those preconceptions would be confirmed – and so they were.

Autocar was first to drive the car, within a fortnight of it being officially announced, and the review read as though it had been written by BMW's own PR team –

DID YOU KNOW?

There was a single M3 Compact produced in 1996, using the standard M3 mechanicals but in the Compact's bodyshell – which was 230mm shorter than the standard car's. This hot Compact was built as a 50th birthday present for German car magazine *Auto, Motor und Sport*, and it could storm from 0-60mph in just 5.2 seconds thanks to a kerb weight a whopping 150kg lighter than its saloon counterpart.

The M Compact remained a one-off, but if BMW had produced a seriously powerful version of its smallest car, it would no doubt have sold strongly.

Some of the colour schemes could be pretty revolting (or drab), but the dashboard of the E46 M3 was as good as anybody ever needed a dashboard to be. (BMW)

the opening line said it all: 'With its handling, looks, aggression and comfort, BMW's new M3 is about to become the benchmark sports saloon.' That issue's cover was equally unequivocal: 'Flat out in the fastest, hairiest, cleverest BMW *ever*' was about as unambiguous as you could get. This was one hell of a car. That first review contained so many glowing references that it is difficult to choose just one passage to sum up just how good they considered the new M3 to be. A good start would be: 'You'll soon start to wonder why anyone else would bother trying to build a rival to such a car, because not only is this the fastest BMW in history, but it could also, just possibly, be the best.'

There were all sorts of reasons for the overwhelmingly positive sentiments towards the new car, but the main ones were the stated performance figures – although these actually proved to be conservative. With a claimed 0–62mph time of 5.2 seconds – an improvement of 0.3 seconds over its predecessor – the new M3 was definitely no slouch. But as was so often the case with BMW's claimed figures, the reality was even better. When *Autocar* tested the M3 against the stopwatch a 0–60mph time of 4.8 seconds was recorded along with a 0–100mph time of just 11.5 seconds. The standing quarter-mile time of 13.3 seconds went with a 50–75mph time that was cut from 5.7 seconds to just 5.4 seconds. According to BMW the

Above: It wasn't just the facia that was inviting, as the whole of the interior was sumptuously trimmed and extremely well equipped. (BMW)

Above: Although the E46 M3 was reasonably discreet, there were plenty of detail touches that hinted at its huge potential. (BMW)

Below: Once the E46 M3 had been introduced, the demise of the E36 M3 suddenly didn't seem such bad news. (BMW)

With 343bhp, the new M3's powerplant enabled the car to sprint from a standing start to 62mph in under five seconds. (BMW)

M3 was also capable of stopping from 62mph in just 2.6 seconds. This was all despite an increase in kerb weight of 40kg (88lb), meaning the E46 M3 tipped the scales at 1,570kg (3,462lb). Increases of 22bhp and 11lb ft of torque explained the improved sprinting abilities – in fact, the car was so quick that it even beat the 400bhp V8 M5, making it the fastest accelerating M car ever.

Naturally, the top speed was still electronically limited to 155mph, but BMW felt that was surely

The E46 M3's engine was fitted with a cast-iron cylinder block for durability. An alloy cylinder head was fitted, and so was Double-VANOS for better high-end power. (BMW)

enough for even the most demanding driver. Yet all this was combined with tractability, practicality and space – it didn't seem as though anybody could ever need anything more than an M3.

The original thinking for the car was that the 4.9-litre V8 normally seen in the M5 would be shoehorned under the M3's bonnet. Such a move would have meant the engine would already be certificated for emissions and a new powerplant wouldn't have to be developed, thus slashing costs. In the end it was felt that a normally aspirated in-line six was the way to go, to fit in with expectations of the brand, and with 106bhp per litre, the M3's normally aspirated engine had a higher specific power output than any car available anywhere in the world. Except of course, buyers cared more about ultimate power rather than specific power, and since Audi's launching of an all-new S4 complete with twin-turbocharged 4.2-litre V8, things have been shaken up somewhat. The S4 may have just one horsepower more than the M3, but the gauntlet has been well and truly thrown down. With the stakes having been raised, no doubt there will be some rethinking going on at Motorsport with regard to the E46 M3's successor. After all, the S4's engine has room for uprating, whereas the M3's powerplant is not far off the limits of development.

Although the engine from the previous generation of M3 was used for the E46, there were just five interchangeable components between the original version of the 3,201cc unit and the new 3,246cc one, which is why this unit carried the new, S54 designation. That 44cc increase was brought about by a 0.6mm enlargement of the bore, but the changes went far deeper than that. The previous engine had been taken to the limits of development, so wholesale changes were called for if any advances were going to be made. The cast-iron bottom end was retained for the sake of durability, although magnesium was considered as an alternative. By remapping the MSS54 engine management system, the rev limit was raised to 8,000rpm. A switchable electronic butterfly control within the throttle intake system allowed a faster response to the accelerator being pressed hard to the floor. By flicking a switch on the centre console the fuelling would be remapped by the management system and at the same time the valving of the rack-and-pinion steering would be adjusted to provide more direct feel.

Few changes were made to the Getrag six-speed manual gearbox between its fitment in the E36 M3 and its installation in the E46, as it was felt that the ratios were suited to the new engine's torque characteristics.

Also, it was strong enough to cope with the 296lb ft of torque that the 3.2-litre engine developed. But in a bid to maximise traction, the differential was changed to a new variable unit developed in conjunction with British engineering specialists GKN. By keeping track of any differences in traction between the rear wheels, it was possible to engage an electronically controlled clutch to vary the lock on the rear wheels to anywhere between zero and almost 100 per cent. The wheel running under less load (such as the inner wheel on a fast bend) would not, therefore, lose drive forces, thus ensuring that the car maintained its forward progress in all situations. This distribution of power between the driven wheels was achieved by a shear pump reading the loss of load on one wheel and generating pressure to a multiple plate clutch. This, in turn, conveyed drive force to the wheel with better grip. In an extreme case the drive force may have been transmitted to just one wheel then, when the difference in wheel speeds decreased, the locking action was reduced. The advantage of all this was a significant increase in handling and driving stability.

Two years of intensive testing meant the rest of the chassis was given a thorough going over. MacPherson struts were retained for the front and at the back was BMW's familiar trapezoidal Z-beam multi-link set-up. To cope with the punishment the car was bound to get,

a lot of the suspension components were strengthened and in a bid to sharpen responses and reduce unsprung masses, a lot of the suspension components, such as track control arms, were cast in aluminium. To help with cornering and also to make the car look more aggressive compared with the standard 330Ci, the ride height was reduced by 15mm at the front and 10mm at the rear. Cornering abilities were also improved by stiffening the springs and dampers and by fitting firmer bushes to the suspension at both ends of the car.

With such huge performance available, it was natural that BMW would fit a monster braking system, along with plenty of electronic aids to help prevent anyone from exceeding the car's incredibly high limits, so that they didn't end up wrecking the car and themselves. Ventilated discs were fitted all round, although, unusually, the rear units at 328mm were fractionally larger than those at the front, which were 325mm in diameter. The calipers were cast in aluminium and anti-lock brakes were standard from the outset. Other circuitry that helped keep the car on the road included dynamic stability control, which reduced engine power and braked individual wheels if the sensors detected a

To keep the power in check, the M3 had a chassis that was on a par with the best available elsewhere. Huge attention to detail had been paid. (BMW)

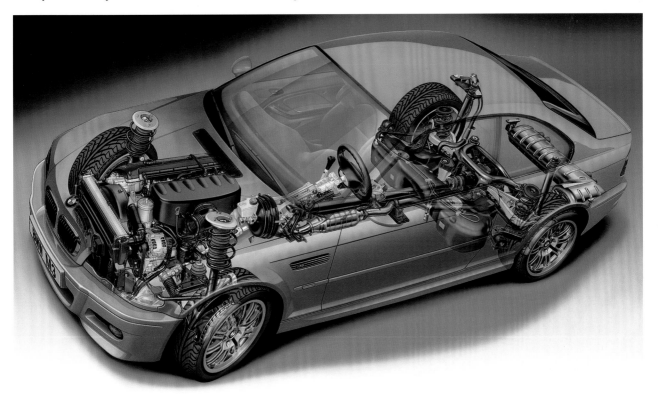

loss of traction at any corner. Cornering brake control also monitored each corner, and if the brakes were being applied too hard while the car was changing direction, the braking would be eased to ensure that the wheel didn't lock.

Whereas the E36 M3 had always attracted criticism for being too understated – especially after the E30 version – the E46 couldn't be the victim of such accusations. The track was 60mm wider, and that was obvious just by looking at the bulging wheelarches. The 18in wheels were wrapped in 40-series tyres at the back and 45-series at the front – an unusual touch being the opportunity for the owner to specify whether they wanted Michelin Pilots or Continental Contact Sports. There were styling touches all around the car that emphasised its sporting pretensions. Behind the front wheelarches was an air vent emblazoned with the M logo – a touch which was intended to echo the one seen on the classic 3.0CSi Batmobile of the early 1970s. The front and rear bumpers were far more chunky than those of the standard car and the huge air intake within the front spoiler, complete with black mesh grille, hinted at the hugely powerful engine hiding behind. The bonnet incorporated a power bulge that somehow managed to proclaim loudly that it wasn't just for show, while at the same time being reasonably discreet and poking menacingly out of the rear valance was a pair of

The brakes were the biggest ever fitted to the 3-Series, with stopping power that would have been unimaginable when the first M3 had been seen a decade and a half earlier. (BMW)

twin tailpipes which had become an M trademark.

Inside it was no less dramatic, with sculpted seats front and rear – seats which were unique to the M3 and which were cosseting and supportive even when the car was being driven flat out. Trim choices were between Alcantara and leather and so that wood trim didn't have to be specified there was also the option of brushed alloy inserts along the dash and on the doors. A multi-function three-spoke steering wheel was standard and a neat touch, which was also seen on the M5, was a rev counter incorporating a series of warning lights which adjusted the red line according to the engine's temperature. But perhaps the prize for most frivolous interior appointment should go to the gearknob, which lit up when the headlights were switched on. Also seen in the M Roadster, this showed the gearbox shift pattern once the sun had gone down.

BMW had been stung by criticisms of the SMG-equipped E36 M3 – but despite this, half of all M3s were ordered with this gearbox. So when the transmission was offered in the E46 from Summer 2001, it received a comprehensive overhaul. Dubbed SMG II, the second generation of this transmission incorporated Drivelogic, which offered 11 different driving programmes such as 'relaxed', 'winter' and 'very sporting'. The fastest gear changes could be underatken in just 80 milliseconds and shift lights in the rev-counter display lit up to indicate the optimum shift point. This time round BMW had got it just right, with the system receiving rave reviews – it would be much harder to improve on SMG II than it had been to make the first version better.

The earlier SMG-equipped cars had sold well despite the system not being well received by critics. The new M3 had SMG II instead, which was far better developed. (BMW)

M3 cabrio

The lack of success BMW had had in selling the E36 M3 saloon meant no four-door version of the E46 M3 would be built. A convertible was definitely on the cards however, and that arrived in Summer 2001. Mechanically the same as the M3 Coupé, the Convertible carried a 100kg weight penalty over its fixed-head sibling – but it was still able to sprint from a standing start to 62mph in little more than five seconds while the top speed was still electronically limited to 155mph. The folding roof was the same as the one used on lesser 3-Series convertibles, which meant pressing a button was as much effort as it took to either raise or retract it. Safety was taken care of courtesy of twin front airbags and side airbags as well, while there were pop-up roll over bars which were activated within 0.11 seconds of the sensors detecting that a roll over was imminent.

When *Autocar* tested the drop-top M3 the verdict was: 'Compared with the standard Coupé, the Convertible loses convincingly in every area. But so complete is the normal M3, that robbing its chassis of 15 per cent of its ability still leaves it with more than most cars ever had.' That was echoed elsewhere – cutting the roof off a coupé will always compromise its handling, but when it has such huge talents to begin with, the typical driver is hardly going to notice any compromises having been made.

M3 GTR

The biggest major-league sports car series in America at the time of the M3 GTR's launch, was the ALMS

The third-generation Convertible M3 lost little in the driving experience over its Coupé sibling, despite a large weight penalty. (BMW)

(American Le Mans Series). Dominated by the Porsche 911, all cars entered in the series had to be based on a road-going production model. So essentially, anyone wanting to buy their own example of an ALMS-entered car had to be able to order one from a dealer. Yet when the V8-engined M3 GTR first started to win races in the 2001 series, it wasn't actually available for anyone to buy – so it just had to be by the end of the year. But by

The most outrageous M3 (and probably BMW) ever was the GTR, which dominated the American Le Mans Series in 2001. It had a V8 engine and 450bhp. (BMW)

The E46 wasn't the first 3-Series range to spawn an M3 GTR version, as the E36 had also done so. This is Johnny Cecotto racing in 1993. (BMW)

2002, the GTR's racing days were over, after it had taken Porsche to the cleaner's. A roadgoing car had been shown, with a price of 250,000 euros (£157,000) attached to it, but no GTRs were sold – and at such a high cost it is doubtful whether any would have been, even if the car had been available.

By using carbon-fibre body parts and by completely foregoing any comfort equipment, the two-seater M3 GTR was one of the most extreme cars ever to come out of the M division. Without fuel or passengers the GTR tipped the scales at 1,100kg (2,425lb) and when this was mixed with a 4.0-litre V8 developing in excess of 450bhp, the result was predictably explosive. Such power outputs were only available when the car was built to circuit specification – road cars had to be fitted with silencers and emissions reduction technology which reduced power output to a more sober 350bhp – still enough to guarantee electrifying acceleration, but not that far removed from the 343bhp of the standard car.

The road version of the M3 GTR was kept technically as close as possible to the racing version. Apart from the lightweight V8 engine, this meant dry sump lubrication, a six-speed gearbox, a two-disc sports clutch and a variable M differential lock. For weight reduction all versions of the GTR featured a roof, the rear spoiler and front and rear aprons all made of carbon-fibre reinforced plastic (CRP). The extended front and rear apron as well as the rear spoiler optimised the aerodynamics and additional cooling slits in the bonnet ensured the high-performance powerplant didn't self destruct because of high underbonnet temperatures. The BMW M3 GTR featured suspension that was both much lower and much stiffer, which favoured handling over ride. The compact V8 allowed optimum weight distribution which, together with the 19in sports wheels, guaranteed outstanding handling. So it was a great shame that no GTRs were ever built for the road – although whether or not anybody would have stumped up the asking price is another matter.

The M3 CSL

With BMW struggling to meet demand for the E46 M3 in the spring of 2003, the company announced an even more desirable (and faster) model – the M3 CSL. The name harked back to the classic CSL coupés of the 1970s – cars which were seen as among the most desirable at the time, thanks to their exclusive prices, small production runs and success on the race track. Aimed at the driver who prized performance above all else, the CSL was not only 110kg (243lb) lighter than the standard car, but also 17bhp more powerful, with no less than 360bhp on tap. The weight loss was achieved by using CRP for some of the panels such as the front spoiler, roof and rear spoiler, so that the end result was a kerb weight of 1,385kg (3,054lb) and a power-to-weight ratio of 260bhp/tonne. The engine retained its 3.2-litre capacity and the 360bhp peak power figure was achieved at a monumental 7,900rpm while at 3,000rpm lower down the scale the peak torque figure was achieved, a healthy 273lb ft being at the driver's disposal. These were numbers that were high enough to allow the car to scorch from a standing start to 62mph in 4.9 seconds and on to 125mph (200kmh) in just 16.8 seconds. As was common practice for BMWs, the M3 CSL was artificially restricted to 155mph (250kmh), but with the restrictor removed the car could probably have travelled at least another 30mph (48.27kmh) faster.

But the M3 CSL wasn't just about straight-line speed – being able to corner at indecently high velocities was also part of the recipe and to that end BMW had its sights on the Nürburgring Northern Circuit lap record. It was this 20.8-mile (33.5kmh) circuit in the Eifel mountains which BMW had used to hone each of its M cars and the target of eight minutes for the M3 CSL meant the car had to be pretty special indeed. Although ultimate speed is essential for such exploits, being able to carry that speed through the bends is even more important and to that end the aerodynamics of the M3 CSL were improved over the standard car. The front air dam and rear diffuser ensured reduced lift at each end of the car and the lighter roof (albeit by just 6kg/13lb) helped to lower the centre of gravity slightly. Weight savings were made elsewhere in the M3 CSL by adopting glassfibre thermoplastics in the construction of various parts – technology that is usually reserved for aerospace applications. And to top it all off, like the standard M3, the CSL version was fitted with an aluminium bonnet and extra-thin glass for the rear window. Equipment levels were also reduced to keep weight down, and although air conditioning and a radio weren't fitted, they could be specified at no extra cost. Other equipment losses included the heated seats

which were now glassfibre reinforced plastic with manual adjustment. Some felt the inclusion of rear seats in such a car as the M3 CSL was tantamount to heresy, but they were fitted, and like the front units they were individual buckets trimmed with lightweight upholstery. Even the carpeting was chosen for its light weight, and to reduce inertia even further, some of the interior panelling was carbon-fibre.

The standard M3 chassis was hardly lacking, but the reduced weight of the CSL called for improvements to be made to the suspension, brakes and steering. There were shorter front springs while both spring and damper rates were also revised. Aluminium track control arms were used at the rear to complement those at the front, these using ball bearings in place of the previous rubber items, ensuring the car's directional stability was improved in the most extreme driving. The rack-and-pinion steering was made a little sharper by decreasing the ratio slightly and the brakes were beefed up at the front, although the rear ventilated discs were the same size as those of the standard M3. This meant they were 20mm thick and 328mm in diameter, whereas the front units were 28mm thick and 345mm across – naturally the anti-lock braking system was also tweaked a bit to reduce stopping distances even further. In normal road driving these brakes were equipped with high-performance pads, but if the car was to be taken on to a track it was possible to buy even higher specification pads which would bring the stopping distances tumbling down. BMW claimed that using these ultra-high spec pads, it was possible to pull the car up from 62mph (100kmh) in just 34m (111ft) in just 2.5 seconds. Compare this with the official stopping distance in the *Highway Code* of 73m (240ft) and you can see the CSL's braking system wasn't lacking.

The icing on the cake was a new set of wheels and tyres that went beyond anything available for the regular M3; 19in rims were fitted all round and although wheels with the same diameter could be specified for the standard M3, those fitted to the CSL were a whopping 11kg (24lb) lighter. At the front these were 8in wide while the rear units were an inch wider, all wrapped in extra sticky Michelin Pilot Sport Cup tyres which were developed specially for the M3 CSL. The rear tyres were among the lowest profile ones available, as they were 265/30 ZR 19 units. At the front they weren't quite such a low-profile being 235/35 ZR 19, but like those fitted at the back, they used an asymmetric tread pattern.

To make best use of the reduced weight and improved suspension, the power of the engine was increased and the rev limit taken up to 8,000rpm. To allow the powerplant to breathe more easily an entirely new carbon-fibre reinforced plastic air intake system was fitted along with much larger intake manifolds. Feeding all this was a huge air scoop on the left-hand side of the front air dam and to keep things running smoothly, a faster computer was installed which could make quicker calculations regarding fuelling and ignition. Spicier camshafts and modified valves helped to remove burnt gases from the cylinders as efficiently as possible while the exhaust system was constructed of thinner steel than usual to keep the weight down. The result of all this was a specific power output of 111bhp per litre – a figure which no other normally aspirated production six-cylinder engine could match, and one with which very few powerplants of any configuration could compete.

Having created what would probably be the ultimate

With reduced weight and increased power, the M3 CSL was BMW Motorsport at its best – although it carried a hefty price premium over the standard car. (BMW)

incarnation of the M3 six-cylinder engine, it made perfect sense to produce a transmission to go with it that was equally special. The sequential manual gearbox was the obvious starting point, and this was fitted as standard to the M3 CSL, but some changes were made along the way to make it a little bit more special. Although the ratios could be changed by using the standard paddle shifts or gearstick, as in the standard installation, in the CSL it was possible to allow the car to do the changing of its own accord when attempting a full-bore acceleration run. All the driver had to do was press the acceleration assistant button and once they had floored the throttle the next ratio in the sequence would automatically be selected at just the right moment – before the engine was about to hit the red line. The gadgetry didn't end there however because an extra refinement included in the CSL's multi-function steering wheel was a feature called M Track mode. This gave the driver the opportunity to select a higher level of dynamic stability control activation which allowed the car to be driven right up to its physical limits before any electronics intervened to keep the vehicle from joining the scenery.

The special edition M3s

M318iS

Whereas BMW Motorsport tends to make cars go very quickly while keeping their appearance very understated, the M318iS of 1994 did just the opposite. It looked rather more potent than an M3 saloon yet under the bonnet was the same 16-valve 1.8-litre engine normally seen in a 318iS Coupé. Along with a ridiculously overstated rear spoiler there were more aggressive bumpers front and rear, a blacked out grille and driving lamps set into the front spoiler. Inside, things were equally indiscreet with, for a BMW, flamboyantly trimmed bucket seats and a chunky three-spoke steering wheel.

Despite this showy exterior, the M318iS was powered by a standard 140bhp four-cylinder engine, which developed 127lb ft of torque. This was mated to a five-speed manual gearbox and the resultant performance figures were a top speed of 133mph (214kmh) and a 0–60mph time of 9.9 seconds – hardly seriously quick. The real problem with the M318iS was that its wider tyres and stiffer suspension made everyday driving quite tiresome although the handling was sharp and the brakes very good. Demand within the German market was strong for the car and consequently few cars were sold in other countries – all M318iS production was left-hand drive.

M3 GT

To comply with the 1995 Le Mans regulations, BMW produced 406 examples of the M3 GT for sale in European markets at the end of 1994. Officially they were built with left-hand drive only, although it has been claimed that 50 right-hand drive cars were built. There was no choice of colours inside or out, with dark green paintwork only, and the M3 GT was a more focused driver's car than the regular M3. It featured suspension that was stiffer and lower than standard, along with aerodynamic tweaks such as more prominent front and rear spoilers, the former incorporating a splitter. The 2,990cc engine was uprated to produce a heady 295bhp and although the car was luxurious, its weight was reduced marginally over the standard car thanks to the use of kevlar for some of the interior trim – although any gains really were tiny.

M3 GT2

Built to mark the end of E36 M3 production, the M3 GT2 differed little from the standard production car. That means it featured the same 321bhp 3.2-litre straight-six with suspension and brakes which were the same as on any standard car. Only 50 were made and when launched in 1998, it was known as the M3 Coupé Special Edition – retrospectively, it became known as the M3 GT2.

Although the car wasn't altered mechanically, the interior was uniquely trimmed with red leather inserts in seats that were mainly covered in anthracite Alcantara. The gearlever gaiter and steering wheel featured red stitching and the exterior paint scheme was Imola Red. An electric sunroof was standard and along with a Harmon Kardon six-speaker hi-fi there were few changes to the standard car's specification.

M3 Lightweight

Within a couple of months of the introduction of the M3 GT, in January 1995, the M3 Lightweight arrived, for sale exclusively in the USA. That market already had its own road version of the M3, which was equipped to comply with federal emissions regulations, meaning a drop in power to 240bhp. Although relatively little could be done to increase the power significantly, by reducing the weight substantially, a sharper handling car could be produced. As a result of ditching the air conditioning, sunroof, radio and sound insulation, while adopting aluminium doors, a useful 91kg (200lb) was lost, despite the addition of body stiffening to sharpen the handling further. The result of this work led to a 0–60mph time of around 5.8 seconds, despite no increase in power. Such a quick time was important because the car wasn't really intended for road use – this was one for the track.

To ensure the car stayed on the circuit, there were various aerodynamic additions to increase downforce. These included GT-style spoilers at both the front and rear, with the front one incorporating a splitter that could be removed for street use. The alloy wheels differed from the standard units by being double-spoked, but the running gear was standard M3, with its 3.23:1 back axle ratio. Inside there were lightweight seats and trim with carbon fibre detailing to highlight the lightweight nature of the car. By the time production ended, 85 examples of the M3 Lightweight had been made, although strangely, BMW's records show that 31 extra cars were built, but where they were sold has never been stated.

M3-R

It wasn't just Europe and the USA which had more focused versions of the M3, as Australia got one, especially for racing and named the M3-R. Unlike the cars available elsewhere, the M3-R was only for use on the track, with just 15 being made in total, four of which were works cars. But it wasn't the BMW works team which campaigned them – it was Australian privateer Frank Gardner's BMW M Team which raced these cars. The 3-litre engine was tuned to give 326bhp and 200kg was shed by losing the spare wheel, some interior trim, the sound proofing and the tools in the boot. The suspension was uprated to optimise the handling and four-pot calipers were fitted front and rear, while the clutch was also strengthened. To help keep the car on the ground there was a bigger rear wing and a front splitter styled on the one fitted to the GT2. Finishing off the car were BBS 17in alloy wheels.

Canadian Limited Edition

With the exception of a 240bhp 3-litre US-spec engine, each of the 45 individually numbered M3s imported by BMW into Canada in 1994 carried the same specification as standard European-market left-hand-drive M3s.

Chapter Five

The Compact

When BMW launched its Compact in 1994, there were many who wondered if the company was selling its soul. Having taken years to build a reputation that was far removed from the bubble cars of the 1950s, the thought of a BMW as cheap as the Compact was a step too far in the eyes of many observers. But although many rival makers were moving upmarket, like BMW they were also producing cheaper cars as well, in a bid to hook buyers earlier on. By selling a Compact to somebody who would otherwise buy a Golf, the thinking was that when this car was sold the owner would then move up to a 3-Series, possibly followed by a 5-Series – and maybe beyond.

Although the E36 Compact was clearly derived from the 3-Series, it carried over relatively little from that model. In fact, it probably would have made more sense to have badged the car as a '2-Series' because it was significantly smaller than the other bodystyles in the 3-Series range, and it was also marketed as a premium small hatch. Although it was recognisably an E36, it was only forward of the A-pillars that the metal had any similarity to the saloon and with the exception of different headlamps which were 40 per cent more efficient, there were no differences between the two cars ahead of the windscreen. But from there back it was pretty much all new, and although the car looked far shorter than the rest of the 3-Series range, the Compact actually retained the 2,700mm wheelbase that the saloon, Coupé and Convertible used. The doors were taken from the Coupé (although they weren't frameless as on that car) and between the saloon and the hatchback there was a difference in length of 223mm.

The Compact was launched as a premium small car, which counted models such as the Volkswagen Golf and Alfa Romeo 145 among its rivals. (LAT)

DID YOU KNOW?

The production E36 Compact was preceded by a series of prototypes which featured far sleeker lines. The hatch was at a much shallower angle suggesting the car would be a 2+2 rather than a practical four-seater. Front-wheel drive prototypes were built, but BMW decided only rear-wheel drive would be offered, then the project was canned in favour of the more practical car that made it to the showroom.

Because the car was a BMW it had to be sporty and exceptionally well made, but it was a small hatch so it also had to be practical with decent space efficiency. To that end the rear seats folded down to provide a usefully sized load bay and the boot floor was flat to maximise the carrying capacity. The complicated suspension introduced on the E36 would have eaten into the available space far too much, which called for a big compromise in the shape of outdated suspension technology from the E30. The use of such an old design led to criticism of the car's handling, which had clearly been sacrificed in favour of improved practicality – but as the car would be a style statement for image-conscious young buyers, this was the balance that BMW felt was right.

It wasn't just the platform which was changed for the introduction of the new bodystyle, as the Compact also received a new dashboard which was inspired by the 5-Series and 7-Series. It was instantly recognisable as a BMW, with excellent ergonomics and thanks to lower production costs it was possible to sell the Compact for the lowest possible price. After all, the premium small hatch market was beginning to grow with Audi working on its own contender, the A3, which was due to be introduced not long after. But unlike the A3 – and every other car that could potentially lay claim to being a hot hatch – the Compact retained the rear-wheel drive layout of every other BMW. This led the way to versions of the car with ever more powerful engines, although unusually for BMW, there were no six-cylinder Compacts available at first, the choice being between 316i, and 318Ti. Within a year however, there would also be a 90bhp 318tds, powered by a 1,665cc four-cylinder engine.

The 316i featured a 105bhp 1,895cc powerplant while the 318Ti was fitted with a 140bhp version of the same engine. This unit had first been seen back in 1988 and for its introduction in the Compact, there were some refinements to keep it up to date. One of the most important of these was BMW's individual control intake manifold (ICIM), but there were also cylinder-specific knock control and solid state ignition thrown into the mix for good measure. The ICIM system varied the intake manifold length so that at low revs it took longer to increase torque while at high revs its length was reduced to increase top-end power. But it wasn't just about increasing power and torque – by fitting roller rockers to the engine, efficiency could be increased so that fuel consumption could be reduced. This worked by reducing friction between the camshaft and rocker

Although the Compact was a small car, its dash was on a par with the more expensive models in the BMW range, which meant it was excellent. This is a 318Ti. (LAT)

arm surfaces, and BMW claimed that at low to medium engine speeds, fuel consumption could be reduced by as much as six per cent.

Reduced running costs were also important, not least because the Compact was at the budget end of the BMW range, and buyers were going to be attracted to the car predominantly because of its pricing. To this end, a chain was used to drive the camshaft, in place of the belt previously fitted. This lasted the life of the engine, just like the poly V-belt which was used to drive the engine ancillaries, where previously, a conventional V-belt had been used, necessitating periodical replacement. The move to a solid state distributor meant reduced running costs for the ignition system and to top it all off there was BMW's service interval indicator which allowed the mileage between services to be extended if the car was driven in a leisurely manner.

Both of the four-cylinder petrol engines available in the Compact were equipped with 16 valves and in the case of the 318Ti, the 'Ti' badge was chosen to hark back to the 1960s and '70s when cars such as the 2002Ti were the sporty BMW options. Although in the mid-1990s, when diesels were generally still seen as anything but sporty, for a car to succeed in the all-important European markets, an oil-burning option had to be offered. Market share was important, and buyers of premium small cars were usually interested in minimising running costs. That is why the 318tds was a part of the line-up and although it wasn't especially

At first, only four-cylinder Compacts were available, and by the end of E36 production, the only six-cylinder Compacts would be left-hand drive examples, like this 328Ti. (LAT)

popular in the UK, European markets found it far more palatable on account of the much lower cost of diesel fuel over petrol, along with the inherent added frugality.

Mated to these four-cylinder engines was a choice of five-speed manual gearbox or four-speed automatic. Those who preferred to shift gears themselves got a unit with a direct-drive fifth gear, rather than the overdrive favoured by many other car makers, largely on account of the relative lack of torque of the petrol engine, as it had just 110lb ft available. The diesel was slightly better as it generated up to 129lb ft of torque, but this still wasn't really enough to endow the car with strong acceleration when cruising, so a shorter top gear ratio made perfect sense – even if fuel consumption suffered slightly as a result. Anyone opting for the automatic gearbox got a transmission with three available modes. The Economy setting changed up earlier and improved fuel economy while the Sport setting changed up later in the rev range, to make the most of the available torque. There was also the option of a Manual over-ride, which held the transmission in a particular ratio, which was especially useful for anyone driving in slippery conditions who didn't want the gearbox to suddenly swap ratios.

In common with all BMWs, safety was high on the agenda while the car was being developed. Ahead of the A-pillars the Compact was structurally the same as any other E36, including the windscreen angle of 61 degrees, but after that it was all new. The car's crumple zones were engineered to withstand a frontal impact at 35mph (56kmh) and a rear or side impact at 30mph (48kmh). The monocoque featured extra-large load-bearing members and where these met there were reinforced intersection points – all designed using the latest CAD technology. The chassis legs were of octagonal construction to help reduce repair costs in the event of a shunt and the bodyshell was stiffened to minimise intrusion into the passenger space if the worst happened. To aid this there were side impact bars in the doors and all the hinges and locks were reinforced to make sure that nothing broke away in an accident. The C-pillars were strengthened and so was the rear-most section of the floorpan. BMW also emphasised the safety aspects of the Compact's suspension – which was interesting, considering that the rear set-up was from the previous generation of 3-Series (the E30). It was clear that outdated summed it up rather better than cutting-edge. The central arm configuration usually seen in the 3-Series was ditched in favour of semi-trailing arms with separate springs and dampers. To take the reduced length and mass into account these were retuned to adjust the damping characteristics – it went some way to addressing the problem, but there was only so much that could be done with such an old suspension layout. At the front the same suspension system was used that any full-size 3-Series buyer would be familiar with and the twin-circuit brake system was equipped with Teves anti-lock brakes as standard on all models.

As soon as the Compact went on sale there were thousands of column inches given to it by the journalists. BMW had long been the darling of the motoring press and to some the company could do no wrong – while others were convinced this was the beginning of the end. Everyone was agreed on one thing – it was the world's only rear-wheel-drive small hatchback and as a result it enjoyed dynamics that none of its rivals could offer. But opinions were less clear cut on whether or not the rear suspension adopted was a compromise too far. At the end of 1994, *Car* magazine put a 316i Compact up against a Volkswagen Golf GTi, and although the BMW was judged the better buy overall if quality, image and equipment were the priorities, when it came to driving fun it was definitely beaten not only by the Golf but also by the Peugeot 306 XSi. When *Autocar* had performed the same test earlier in the year, once more it was the Compact which was judged to be the best car overall. This was despite the Golf being better for practicality,

Rear-seat space wasn't especially generous, but for anyone who rarely used the back seats, the Compact was the small hatch of choice; here is the 328Ti. (LAT)

DID YOU KNOW?

In 1996, an M version of the Compact was created to celebrate the 50th birthday of German car magazine *Auto, Motor und Sport*. The car was never intended for production, but by the time the E46 had been introduced in 2002, rumours started which suggested BMW was going to produce an M Compact after all. Power was to come from the 230bhp 3.0-litre straight-six usually seen in the 330i, but it all came to nothing when BMW confirmed that no such car would ever make it to the showroom.

driving fun on challenging roads and performance – the latter being no surprise given its extra displacement under the bonnet.

For many buyers it didn't really matter too much about the driving experience – the purchase of a Compact was a style statement. BMW fuelled that by offering bespoke interior and exterior colours through its Personal Line service, which meant there were nine options for the cabin and 13 for the paintwork, to give 152 combinations. By also allowing owners to specify equipment from the options list there was no need for two Compacts to be the same – exactly what image-conscious buyers wanted. Because of a high starting price for even the basic 316i, BMW had no choice but to include equipment for which rival makers charged extra – electric mirrors, heated door locks and washer nozzles were all standard, along with power-assisted steering. However, even the 318Ti came with steel wheels – BMW knowing that most buyers would pay extra for something that made such a difference to the car's looks, so there was no way alloy wheels would be included in the standard package.

The Compact offered plenty of practicality, being a small hatch. But the chassis was compromised in the bid to make it as space-efficient as possible. (BMW)

The six-cylinder Compact

It took three years for BMW to launch a six-cylinder version of the E36 Compact, with the 323Ti not appearing until 1997. Hailing back to the 2002Ti of two decades earlier, the new car was badged 323Ti, for *Turismo Internationale* – a reference to production touring car racing. The intention from the outset of the Compact project was to stick with four-cylinder engines only. But as ultra-quick small hatches started to proliferate (such as the Golf V6 and Audi S3) BMW quickly realised that a six-cylinder Compact, even if produced and sold in small numbers, was worth doing. The company didn't go the whole hog though as even when the car was put into production, right-hand drive cars weren't built. The reasoning behind this was that the extra expense incurred with the homologation was unnecessary because BMW could sell all the cars it could make, just by sticking with left-hand drive. After all, just 6,000 units a year were envisaged – although BMW GB reckoned they could sell up to half that quantity if the steering wheel was on the right-hand side.

The M52 engine was used in 2,494cc form, and although the Compact's rear suspension had always been compromised, the chassis as a whole could easily cope with more power. To make the most of the extra power the chassis was tweaked, including the ride height being lowered by 15mm and the adoption of 16in alloy wheels while the suspension was stiffened to give a sportier ride. Whereas the four-cylinder cars were

DID YOU KNOW?

In December 1995 BMW released for sale in Germany a variant of the Compact called the 316g. Essentially the same as the standard car, this was built to run on compressed natural gas, which meant it had a second fuel tank for the fuel and a changeover switch to swap between fuels. The result of the technology was a reduction in CO_2 of 20 per cent and hydrocarbons were cut by 80 per cent, but the car was very expensive and only a few were sold.

fitted with solid discs at the front, the 323Ti had ventilated disc brakes with disc brakes also fitted at the rear. With typical BMW attention to detail, the battery was relocated to the boot – until now having been fitted at the front of the car, but the heavier six-cylinder engine would have made the car nose-heavy. The result of all this development was a car which at a stroke eradicated the shortcomings of the other Compacts. The 170bhp and 177lb ft of torque, when combined with the much more fluid chassis, made the car dynamically superb – some magazines even made comparisons with the M3 on account of its significantly lighter weight. Performance was also much better, with a top speed of 144mph and a 0–60mph time of just 7.6 seconds – this was what the Compact should have been about all along, yet relatively few markets would see this car. Not only was this a waste of a really good car, but it was also a marketing mistake that BMW wouldn't repeat when the next generation of Compact arrived.

Although the six-cylinder E36 Compact wasn't built in right-hand-drive form, from January 1999 the entry-level model was fitted with a 1.9-litre engine for added zest. (BMW)

Something none of the Compact's rivals offered was a huge range of optional colours inside and out to allow greater personalisation. (BMW)

The E36 Open Air special edition Compact was built from Summer 1999 and featured cross-spoke alloy wheels, an electrically operated folding roof and air conditioning. (BMW)

E46 Compact

The arrival of an all-new Compact in Summer 2001 was well overdue. Although BMW seemed capable of selling anything with its badge on it, the reality was that the Compact was doing the company's image no favours.

The car had its fair share of plaudits, but it was let down by that rear suspension. To be fair, it wasn't so much that the car was bad – it was more a case of it being overshadowed by its finer handling saloon, Coupé, Convertible and Touring brothers. The car had done well for BMW, with over 400,000 being sold around the world during its seven-year lifespan – enough to account for 21 per cent of all 3-Series sales. Of those, 37,000 were in the UK market – which meant more than 5,000 British buyers were snapping them up each year. Although such quantities might not sound that great, two-thirds of those buyers went on to buy another BMW – which was exactly why BMW had introduced the car in the first place.

At first, just the 1.8-litre and 192bhp 2.5-litre engines were available – whereas the six-cylinder E36 Compact hadn't been sold with right-hand drive, BMW learned its lesson with the E46 Compact and from the beginning a six-pot version with the steering wheel on the right-hand side was offered. The 1.8-litre car carried a 316Ti badge while the 2.5-litre car was known as the 325Ti: by October 2001 there would also be petrol and diesel-powered versions, both of which featured 2.0-litre engines. The 320td used the common-rail 1,995cc

The all-new E46 Compact of 2001 was just what BMW needed – here at last was a small car from the company, with the chassis it deserved. (BMW)

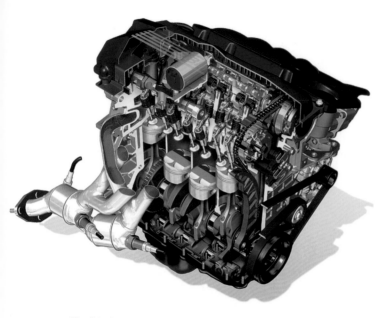

The E46 Compact was the first BMW ever to be equipped with a Valvetronic powerplant, which significantly improved engine efficiency. (BMW)

four-cylinder engine that had already been seen in the 320td saloon and Touring, while the 318Ti featured a Valvetronic-equipped petrol-powered engine with the same capacity and configuration as its diesel sibling. The Valvetronic technology had first been seen on the 316Ti, and it was a revolutionary system in that it allowed a 10 per cent increase in power (to 115bhp) but with a decrease in fuel consumption – and hence emissions – of the same amount. The Double-VANOS system previously seen in the M3 was also fitted to the

This time around, BMW did not make the mistake of failing to offer a six-cylinder engine – a 325Ti E46 could be bought and it received rave reviews. (BMW)

316Ti, and thanks to such innovations, the car developed a healthy 115bhp, which made the car good for 125mph (200kmh).

It wasn't just innovations such as Valvetronic and VANOS which enabled the 316Ti's new engine to excel – the powerplant was a clean-sheet design which incorporated several fundamental principles to maximise efficiency. The first of these was an open-deck crankcase which reduced the resistance of coolant flow, thus allowing the use of a much smaller water pump – as a result the efficiency gain was over 60 per cent. The block itself was made from aluminium, and it used a ladder frame which connected the crankcase and sump to make the whole structure much more rigid than usual, to further reduce vibration. By mounting all ancillaries directly to the crankcase, vibration could be reduced even further, although hydraulic engine mounts were retained to keep things even smoother.

Keeping refinement levels high was only part of the brief with the new powerplant – allowing it to run as well as possible with minimal maintenance was also important. To this end there was an anti-knock control which ensured any fuel grade between 87 and 99 octane was suitable and by equipping each cylinder with its own coil, maintenance to the ignition system could be reduced. Hydraulic valve adjustment was expected in any engine by this stage, so this was incorporated along with roller bearings for the valve train – which not only made the engine run more smoothly, but it also reduced fuel consumption. The spark plugs and air filter needed renewing every 62,500 miles and the gearbox and differential were supplied with oil that would never need to be replaced during the car's lifetime. Even the dashboard lighting was maintenance-free, as LEDs were used in place of conventional bulbs so that replacements would never be an issue.

For the first time in a Compact, in place of the standard five-speed manual transmission there was the choice of a five-speed automatic gearbox. Incorporated in this was a system that BMW called adaptive transmission management, which allowed the gearbox to learn the driver's driving style and adapt the shift points accordingly. The technology also ensured that the gearbox didn't change ratios just when it wasn't wanted, such as in a bend and because it was one of BMW's Steptronic transmissions, it also meant there was a sequential manual gearchange facility.

Just like the E36 Compact, the new car featured the same length of wheelbase as its saloon, Coupé and

To give the Compact a different look from the rest of the 3-Series range, it received its own design of nose with four separate headlamps. (BMW)

Touring counterparts, with 2,725mm between the axles. This was an increase of 25mm over the old car, but the overall length was 280mm less than the other models in the 3-Series range because the front and rear overhangs were much shorter, helping to make the car as nimble as possible. Interior space was much better than with the outgoing model, largely because the car grew in every plane – it was 15mm taller, 53mm wider and 52mm longer. All this combined to make it much more competitive against rivals such as the Audi A3 and Volkswagen Golf – but unlike those cars, the Compact was equipped with rear-wheel drive to make it nicer to drive. It also meant that outrageously powerful engines could be fitted more easily, which brought with it rumours of an M Compact as soon as the first official pictures of the car were shown. Sadly, although such a car was considered, it never saw production. Whereas the previous Compact had shared the frontal styling of the other E36 3-Series models, the new car had its own distinctive styling for both the front and rear. Having moved away from separate quad headlamp designs, the Compact moved back to them, with the inner pair much smaller than the outer ones. At the rear there were clear lenses, behind which the lights were mounted individually.

Of course, such issues as maintenance levels, styling and space efficiency paled into insignificance as soon as the first reviewers were handed the keys to the test models. All they cared about was how well it went, so it was just as well that this time BMW had come up with the goods when it came to chassis development. A quicker steering rack made the car more responsive, with just 3.0 turns between locks and the system's

power assistance was adjusted to give greater feel. The adoption of more alloy parts in the suspension meant unsprung weight at each corner could be reduced by 60kg (132lb) and the usual 50:50 front-to-rear weight distribution, along with the retention of rear-wheel drive, gave the car excellent agility. This time around the acclaimed Z-axle was fitted and to help keep the driver out of trouble there were plenty of electronic aids such as traction control, anti-lock brakes, cornering brake control and electronic brake force distribution.

The E46 Compact dash was every bit as good as any BMW driver had come to expect, with clear and logical displays and excellent build quality. (BMW)

The car was also much safer than the E36, with a stronger monocoque, better crumple zones and more airbags to protect the car's occupants in the event of a crash. (BMW)

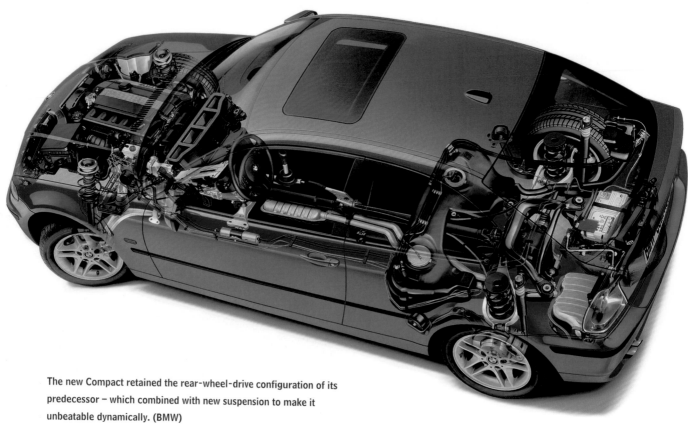

The new Compact retained the rear-wheel-drive configuration of its predecessor – which combined with new suspension to make it unbeatable dynamically. (BMW)

One of the first magazines to review the 325Ti was *Autocar* – a magazine well known for its focus on driver enjoyment rather than practicality. The new arrival should have been just up its street – and it didn't disappoint. With 192bhp to play with and a kerb weight of 1,405kg (3,098lb), although the car was no featherweight, it was still indecently rapid. From a standing start it was possible to hit 60mph in just under seven seconds. The top speed was 144mph (232kmh) but the 181lb ft of torque meant the in-gear times were wonderfully quick – in third gear the 50–70mph (80–113kmh) and 60-80mph (96-129kmh) times were just 4.5 seconds. This meant its main rivals – in the form of the Audi A3 1.8T and Mercedes C230K Sport Coupé were comprehensively beaten. The rear-wheel-drive configuration also endowed the car with excellent handling and as *Autocar* noted: 'when this was combined with gearchange and clutch actions that were positive and sweet, it's a very complete performance.'

The introduction of the 318Ti and 320td Compacts in October 2001 took the three-door 3-Series engine range to four. It also introduced a diesel to the E46 Compact range, and when *Car* magazine tested it they were moved enough to declare: 'the 2.0-litre turbodiesel engine works so well in the Compact that this is the pick of the range so far.' The reason for such a judgment was two-fold – it was rather cheaper than the 325Ti and it was also astonishingly fast yet economical with it. The reason for such strong performance was the 243lb ft of torque and 150bhp on offer – that was more torque than a Porsche Boxster S! Although the 0–60mph time of 8.9 seconds wasn't that quick, it was the in-gear acceleration that was the car's strong point – this car was just made for overtaking.

E46 Compact facelift

At the 2003 Geneva Motor Show, a facelifted Compact was displayed, although changes over its predecessor were generally minimal. The line of the sills was modified and there were minor changes to the contours of the rear panels. Alongside these, new rear lights were used which were of the jewel type then becoming increasingly popular, but the biggest change was the introduction of the 318td, to sit below the 320td which was already available. However, this smaller, four-cylinder engine wasn't introduced into all markets worldwide. At the same time, a new six-speed manual gearbox was introduced, which was fitted as standard to the 320td and the 325Ti. Offering five closely spaced ratios and an overdrive sixth gear, the adoption of the new transmission led directly to a useful four per cent reduction in fuel consumption for the 325Ti. In common with all BMWs equipped with a 2.5-litre or 3.0-litre petrol engine, the 325Ti Compact was also available with the sequential manual gearbox and when the car was equipped with this transmission, even an inexperienced driver could take advantage of scorching acceleration. BMW claimed that even in the hands of a novice, an SMG-equipped 325Ti Compact could sprint from a standing start to 62mph in just 7.1 seconds, by selecting Sport mode.

For 2003, there was a facelifted Compact offered, although changes were minimal. The rear lamp clusters were the most significant external difference. (BMW)

Chapter Six

The Z3 and Z4

Despite BMW's sporting reputation, the company had never taken a serious look at the affordable open-topped sportscar market. Its previous attempt at building a desirable, true sports model was the 507 of 1956–59, and only 254 of those had been built. In the 1970s there were fears of legislation being introduced which would outlaw full convertibles, so mass-market car makers held off unveiling anything that might be affected by such rules. By the 1980s concerns that such laws might be passed began to disappear and so BMW's thoughts turned to building affordable open-topped cars in large numbers. Mazda paved the way with its MX-5, which was launched in 1989 – and BMW wanted to build something that could take on the Japanese sportster.

The Z3's proportions were very sporty, with a long bonnet and short overhangs both front and rear. (BMW)

Although the Z1 had arrived in 1986, it had never been engineered for true mass-production. Indeed, the car went on sale only after it became clear that there was a strong demand for what had been developed as a testbed for the underpinnings of the new 3-Series. This was despite a very high price for what was a small but well-engineered car. When it became known that other car manufacturers would be launching premium two-seater dropheads, BMW realised it needed to develop its new sportscar in quite a hurry. By the time the car was launched in 1997, Mercedes had already unveiled its SLK, MG the F, Porsche its Boxster and both Honda's S2000 and Audi's TT roadster were on the way. The only way of ensuring the car was delivered on time was by using as much as possible from one of the company's existing line up, and considering the compact dimensions of the new car, it would have to be the 3-Series on which the new drophead was based.

It may have been ambitious, but BMW's goal with its new car was to topple the MX-5, which was the world's best-selling sporting roadster. Although the MX-5 had few rivals at first, many more were on the way, and it was especially ambitious because of BMW's position in the marketplace compared with Mazda's. If the German marque wasn't careful, it was in danger of losing its reputation as a maker of exclusive cars if they became too common, but production costs can only be minimised by large production numbers, so it was always going to be a balance between exclusivity and affordability. By basing the car on the 3-Series, both production and purchase costs could be kept to a minimum, which is why the platform of the E36 Compact, which was still going through the development stages, was the ideal candidate.

The main problem with this plan was the fact that the Compact was to be a four-seater, while the car that would be named the Z3 would have just two seats. As a result, the wheelbase that had been developed for the Compact was too long for the Z3, but at least the main mechanical components could be carried over. The Compact shared its wheelbase with the rest of the E36 range, but the important difference was the more compact suspension design which had been adopted because of the intrusive set-up that was used on the saloon and Coupé. Although the semi-trailing arm suspension was compact, it was also based on the outdated design of the E30 – hardly the best starting point for an all-new sportscar. It was for this reason that the Z3 would always be seen as something of a missed opportunity – an all-new car should have set the standard when it came to driving enjoyment. But of course, the reality was that under the skin it wasn't all-new – it was very much a mix and match of old and new parts. To make the Z3 a more sporty drive than the Compact, the front and rear tracks were increased, the former by 7mm and the latter by 14mm. Firmer springs and dampers were fitted and to ensure the car didn't roll too much an uprated anti-roll bar was fitted at each end. To finish off, a more direct steering rack was fitted, although there was still power assistance which some felt took away too much of the feel.

The next issue was sorting out the engine and transmission, although of course BMW wasn't short of suitable powerplants to put in the car. Although the Z3 would span two classes of roadster, at the lower end it would compete with the MX-5. The Mazda had a choice of either 1.6 or 1.8-litre engines, and although BMW could compete directly with these capacities, it was decided that the 1,796cc M43 powerplant should be the smallest unit available. That would be the starting point and because the company had some excellent six-cylinder engines in its armoury, there would also be the chance to buy a much more powerful Z3 later on. To go with the four-cylinder engine there was a choice of close-ratio five-speed manual or four-speed ZF gearboxes. While no true sportscar would have an automatic gearbox, it was clear that many of the people buying the Z3 would be as conscious about badge or style as they were about driving enjoyment – if not more so.

Although the Z3 looked sporty, at first only four-cylinder engines were available – the car promised much, but didn't really deliver in many ways. (BMW)

The Z3 may have been something of a missed opportunity, but at least the car was safe, with plenty of reinforced sections to protect its occupants. (BMW)

With the underpinnings decided, the next stage was to come up with a design that would be a winner. There needed to be a small (but usable) boot and the need for just two seats allowed most of the space behind the A-pillars to be given to the passengers rather than luggage. But despite a four-cylinder engine only being fitted initially, the eventual availability of a six-cylinder unit meant enough space had to be left ahead of the windscreen for the larger powerplant to be fitted. That was no bad thing because the long nose gave the car

The Z3's cabin was very inviting – although the optional leather seen here was a costly extra. (BMW)

more purposeful proportions which were ahead of the MX-5's, as that car was available with four-cylinder power only. As far as the detailing was concerned, the traditional kidney grille had to be incorporated, but there were few other standard BMW styling touches used. The folding roof meant the 'hockey stick' rear pillar couldn't be used and even the rear lights didn't have the corporate look that the saloons had. But one neat touch which did find its way into the design was the quartet of air vents in each of the front wings. Inspired by the 507, there weren't any other styling touches borrowed from BMW's previous classic roadster, which was surprising, considering how popular the retro look was at the time.

Peerless build quality is a hallmark of BMWs, and the company was keen to ensure the Z3 didn't do anything to tarnish that. Although the first cars made at the new Spartanburg plant weren't up to scratch, things were soon rectified to ensure that all was as it should be. During the development stage everything possible was done to make sure the fundamentals were right. The monocoque bodyshell was designed in such a way that scuttle shake would be minimised and bracing around the hood well, within the engine bay and around the bulkheads increased the torsional stiffness. There was even a pair of weights installed in the rear bumper which were designed to cancel out any resonance induced from the torsional vibration of the bodyshell.

Naturally, safety wasn't overlooked with a plethora of active and passive features designed to minimise the chances of injury. Crumple zones were incorporated

BMW pulled off quite a coup by getting the Z3 featured in one of the biggest films of 1995 – the James Bond movie *GoldenEye*. **(BMW)**

front and rear, there were side impact protection beams in the doors and the passenger cell was designed to absorb impact forces in the event of a collision. As well as these measures the windscreen surround, sills and door posts were all strengthened – although no roll hoops were fitted, as the windscreen surround was deemed strong enough to cope in the event of the car becoming inverted. To keep everything in good shape there was a mass of measures to make sure the bodyshell didn't rust, such as 90 per cent of the panels being galvanised and a wax coating injected into all the box sections.

Being a BMW, the Z3 wasn't lavishly equipped, although buyers of even the basic 1.8-litre car could specify all sorts of options to make it more comfortable. Cloth trim was standard although leather could be specified at extra cost. Only the driver had an air bag, but for some extra money the passenger could have one as well. The seats featured electric operation of the fore/aft adjustment but the hood had to be raised and retracted manually – electric operation would arrive later. The hood itself was a neat affair which stowed flush behind the seats beneath a leather-effect tonneau. The rear window could be unzipped to allow better ventilation, and to reduce buffeting at speed there was a mesh wind deflector which could be erected above the stowed roof.

All this attention to detail ensured the Z3 was safe, comfortable, well built and unlikely to suffer from corrosion. But unfortunately, there were also too many compromises and when the car was finally launched at

the Detroit Auto Show in January 1996, it was clear that some fine tuning was necessary for the car to get better reviews. For example, the battery had been located in the boot to maintain the best possible weight distribution. Bearing in mind how much space was available in the engine bay, and how much of that was unused when a mere four-cylinder powerplant was fitted, it was a shame that the already small boot was reduced in size even further by the installation of the battery. Build quality was not up to the usual BMW standards, although it didn't take BMW very long to sort that out. The first official pictures had been released in Summer 1995 with cars starting to roll off the Spartanburg production lines in September of the same year. Although the car wouldn't be seen in the metal until the start of 1996, BMW managed to pull off quite a coup by getting the car to play a starring role in the James Bond film *GoldenEye* the month before it was officially unveiled.

The first cars available were fitted with a 113bhp four-cylinder engine displacing 1,796cc, this engine never being fitted to right-hand drive cars and neither was it available in America. This powerplant was seen as a bit weedy for the US market and when fitted to UK-bound Z3s it would have competed head on with the MGF which had been introduced just before the Z3 made its debut. Initially, only left-hand-drive cars were delivered to customers, from February 1996 and it was

The UK and USA didn't get a 1.8-litre Z3. Instead, the entry-level model was fitted with the 1,895cc four-cylinder engine. (BMW)

another year before right-hand-drive cars were available because of quality control problems at the new factory.

As BMW had just bought the Rover Group, and hence was also then responsible for the MG marque, it made more sense for the Z3 to be marketed a level up from the MG – which also meant it was more expensive than the MX-5, which had been perceived as its greatest rival from the start of the project. Z3s fitted with this 1,796cc engine were pretty basic, despite a premium price. There were no alloy wheels or twin airbags as standard, 15in steel wheels were the order of the day, along with cloth trim and solid paint colours. Owners wanting to spend more on their cars could pay more for metallic paint, an automatic gearbox or leather trim together with anti-lock brakes, air conditioning and sports suspension. Owners who opted for the latter got a car which was equipped with a limited slip differential, a lowered ride height (by 15mm) and consequently sharper handling, but the costs began to add up very quickly. The basic car was already rather pricier than the MX-5, and although it had the BMW badge, it was no quicker. Throw in a dynamic package which, by some testers was seen as inferior to the Mazda's, and

suddenly the extra money being asked for the BMW didn't necessarily make that much sense.

Although the 1.8-litre Z3 didn't make it to the UK or North America, there was still a four-cylinder version sold in both markets. Whereas the old car had been fitted with an eight-valve single-overhead cam four-cylinder engine, the car sold in both the US and UK markets was fitted with a 16-valve double-overhead cam powerplant, but with an extra 99cc to take the capacity to 1,895cc. Using the M44 engine, the Z3 1.9 had a healthy 140bhp available but equipment levels for UK cars were barely any less spartan than they were in the 1.8-litre car. Anti-lock brakes were included in the car's cost, but there was still cloth trim, 15in steel wheels, a manual gearbox, just one air bag and only solid paint finishes. American vehicles got a bit more kit as standard with twin airbags, cruise control, central locking, electric seats and electric windows all included in the car's basic price. Leather trim and metallic paint were extra-cost options, but so was traction control – the first time that BMW had offered such technology on a four-cylinder car.

By the end of 1995, the first cars were available for review, and the overwhelming response from the world's media was how underwhelming the Z3 was. The styling wasn't as cohesive as it should have been, the high price was to be expected, but the build quality certainly wasn't. The handling was okay (but no more) but the grip levels were high – it may have taken a while to get the car up to speed, but at least you could keep it there when, in other cars, you would have to slow down to prevent yourself from coming unstuck. What was really needed was more power, courtesy of a bigger engine – and that was something that buyers didn't have to wait long for.

The six-cylinder Z3

Despite the fact that only four-cylinder Z3s were offered at first, the launch of a six-cylinder version had always been on the cards. The car's engine bay had been designed with the extra length of a straight-six in mind and at the 1996 Geneva Motor Show the world had its first glimpse of the bigger engined Z3 – the 2.8. It wouldn't be until August of that year that the first UK buyers had their cars and at a stroke the bigger engine made the Z3 a rather more appetising proposition than previously. The 2,793cc version of the M52 all-alloy engine had first been seen in the E39 528i in 1995. The E36 328i had been fitted with this unit from 1996, and

with 193bhp on tap, it promised to spice up the Z3 considerably. From a standing start the car could now get to 62mph in just 7.1 seconds and attain a top speed of 135mph (217kmh) – or at least it could with the five-speed manual gearbox that was fitted as standard. For those who preferred to leave the gearchanging to the car itself, a four-speed automatic gearbox was also available.

The extra weight of the six-cylinder engine (41kg/90lb) meant the weight distribution was now an ideal 50:50 front to rear. That in turn meant the suspension had to be tweaked and as a result the settings for the springs, dampers and anti-roll bars were all revised. Wider wheels and tyres were also fitted to allow the power to be put down more easily and to help it corner under power the front track was increased by 2mm while the rear track grew by a whopping 63mm. Although the standard wheels were

It wasn't until a year after the Z3 made its debut that a 2.8-litre six-cylinder version was available. It was better than the 1.9, but still not good enough. (BMW)

BMW's Spartanburg plant

America has long been the most important market for many car makers, and for BMW that was especially the case in the late 1980s and early '90s. Throughout the 1980s BMW had made a lot of money from global sales of its products and by the time the decade was out it was obvious that building a factory in the US would be a prudent thing to do. Not only could BMW not export enough cars to America because of supply problems, but fluctuating exchange rates during the late 1980s had reduced the company's profitability. By building a factory in America, these problems could be addressed in one stroke – and as an added bonus, labour rates in the new factory would be little more than half those of a German counterpart.

BMW had made enough money in the 1980s to pay for a new factory, but it was obviously going to be beneficial if state help was available to soften the blow of setting up a whole new facility. Various sites were chosen, and the winner was a 1,039-acre piece of land in Carolina's Spartanburg. The site was chosen for its good air and rail links, but it was no doubt helped along enormously by the State of Carolina's generous deal involving the land. Valued at $38 million, the state would buy the land and allow BMW to rent it for just a dollar per year, for the first 30 years. BMW could then buy the land at the market price if it wanted to, or continue to rent it at the same rate for another 20 years. Once this half-century had elapsed the company would have to buy the land at its market rate.

It was on 22 June 1992 that BMW announced it had chosen the Spartanburg site, but that was just the start of the operation. As

The Spartanburg factory in the USA opened in 1995 and was capable of producing up to 90,000 cars each year; not that it ever has done. (BMW)

well as building a factory, the workforce had to be selected and trained. Once again, the State of Carolina came to the rescue with an offer to recruit and train the 570 staff required, with no funding necessary from BMW. Anyone wanting a job had to live within 50 miles of the plant, but that didn't stop 65,000 people applying. The first buildings went up in April 1993 and by January 1994 all the essential construction had been completed. The first cars rolled off the production lines on 8 September 1994, although they weren't Z3s. Instead, they were E36 318i kits supplied from Germany, used to test the production facility to make sure that by the time the Z3 was to be built, everything would be in place for smooth production – after all, the Z3 would be built only at Spartanburg, so if there were any problems, there would be no supply of the cars for any of the global markets. On 20 September 1995, the first Z3 was completed, with series production commencing in November of that year. By March 1996, the factory was up to speed although it was still rather a long way off building the 90,000 cars annually that was its planned capacity.

Although BMW had undeniably got a good deal from the State of Carolina, there was one important condition that came with this support. Whereas some parts of BMW's car production in its German factories were largely automated, in Spartanburg it was mainly manual labour which was called upon. Perhaps the best example is the bodyshell production, which in Carolina involved 75 per cent of the welds being performed manually. This compared with more like five per cent in Germany – which was just as well, considering the significantly higher wages needed to pay the staff. Now that production of the Z3 has been discontinued, output has turned to its successor, the Z4.

Above: The Z3, M Roadster and M Coupé were the first cars to be built at Spartanburg, although there were far more manual processes undertaken than BMW was used to. (BMW)

Below: When the Z3 became obsolete, production at Spartanburg was turned to the Z4. (BMW)

From the outside, the six-cylinder Z3s didn't look that different from the four-pot ones – flared wings, twin exhausts and a larger front air scoop were the main distinguishing features. (BMW)

16in in diameter, there was the option of fitting 17in items, which proved to be popular as many of the people buying the new model were rather wealthier than those buying the four-cylinder cars. They needed to be, as the list price had grown substantially and by now the car's main rivals were the Porsche Boxster and Mercedes SLK rather than the Mazda MX-5 and MGF. Discretion was the name of the game with the Z3 2.8 as there was no badging to say this was a more expensive car than its baby brother. Instead, there were flared rear wings, a twin-tailpipe exhaust and a larger air intake at the front. To go some way towards justifying the higher price there was also more equipment fitted as standard – 2.8 buyers could expect a plusher interior with leather trim and wood inserts as standard, and although the very first cars were fitted with a manually operated roof, electric operation became standard very soon after.

By the end of 1996, the press had sampled the first cars, and the difference in reaction over the four-cylinder Z3 was stark. Where the smaller-engined cars lacked power, the 2.8-litre Z3 had ample. The wider track made the car feel far more sure-footed and the lowered and stiffened suspension allowed the car to corner at much higher speeds. Even the looks had been improved because of the more aggressive styling front

and rear – this was definitely worth the extra money over the four-pot car, but there was even better to come.

The M Roadster

Soon after the 2.8-litre Z3 went on sale it was joined by the M Roadster, although BMW announced the car well ahead of when anybody could actually buy one. The car was first seen at the 1996 Geneva Motor Show, but it wouldn't be until the following summer, more than a year after, that it became available in the showroom. Such a lead time was exceptional for BMW, and it happened because, if the company wasn't careful, potential buyers of M cars might have thought BMW was giving up on them. The M5 was already out of production while the new model was being developed, and the M3 was about to be axed, with the new E46 car still several years away. With no M cars available to buy it made sense to make it clear that they were still very much a part of BMW's product plans. American buyers of the car would have to wait even longer because further development was needed on the car destined for that market – in the end it wouldn't be until April 1998 that the first US cars were delivered to their owners. Whereas BMW normally produced its M cars pretty much by hand at its Motorsport division's Garching plant, the M Roadster would have to be produced alongside regular Z3s on the Spartanburg production line in the USA because the cost of shipping between America and Germany would have been prohibitive.

Building the car as a whole was one thing, but the car's engine was quite another. It was much easier to ship ready-built powerplants to Carolina, ready for fitting, than it was to ship bodyshells. So all M Roadster engines were assembled on German production lines before being crated up for despatch. The unit chosen was the only one that BMW could go for: the 3,201cc six-cylinder M3 Evo unit in full 321bhp specification, or at least that was the case for cars not bound for US showrooms. That market got its own engine, just as the M3 had done. In the M Roadster, few changes were made to the engine to distance it from the M3 unit. Perhaps the most significant alteration was the adoption of a pair of twin tailpipes – something which would become a trademark for BMW's M cars and which not only looked rather more purposeful than the standard twin-tailpipe set-up, but which also allowed the engine to breathe more freely. The same MSS50 engine management system was fitted and the car was artificially restricted to 155mph while the 0–62mph sprint could be despatched in just 5.4 seconds.

As was to be expected, there was no automatic transmission option, and because both the six-speed manual gearbox and SMG transmission destined for the M3 Evo were too big to fit into the Z3 bodyshell, the only gearbox available in the M Roadster was the five-speed close-ratio manual which had been fitted to other versions of the Z3. This gearbox was hardly a major shortcoming but unfortunately the low weight of the M Roadster meant BMW couldn't get the electronic traction control system to work properly – it simply could not react fast enough if the wheels started to spin. Instead, more established technology had to be incorporated – a limited slip differential was slotted in, which in the event, was a move that fitted in well with the Motorsport ethos of not fitting too many electronic aids to the car, thus diluting the driving experience.

The Z3's suspension was never going to be good enough for a car carrying the hallowed M badge – it was one of the things that the car had been criticised for since the outset. Although the basic architecture couldn't be changed, there was a lot of scope for improvements through fine tuning. The dampers were stiffened and the springs were shortened while the anti-roll bars were also beefed up. At the same time, the suspension was strengthened substantially so that it could cope with the extra torque over the standard Z3 – in the M Roadster there was 258lb ft available from 3,250rpm. The result of all these changes was an increase of 13mm in the wheelbase and BMW also claimed that the M Roadster's rear subframe was twice as stiff as the one found in the standard car. The chassis development continued with the wheels and tyres, which were 17in in diameter as standard and 7.5in wide at the front: the rears were 9in wide. Wrapped in 225/45 ZR 17 rubber at the front and 245/40 ZR 17 at the back, the five-spoke Roadstar wheels, which were designed specially for the M Roadster looked especially smart.

The power-assisted steering system of the M3 was carried over to the M Roadster, which meant there were 3.2 turns between locks – direct enough to make the car wieldy but not overdirect so it became fidgety at speed. The brakes were also borrowed from the M3,

The M Roadster debuted with the Z3 2.8 in Spring 1996, yet it took a year for the car to appear in showrooms. (BMW)

which ensured the M Roadster was never going to run out of braking capacity, even when driven hard, and the floating-caliper front brakes were part of a system that had anti-lock technology fitted as standard.

Although the M Roadster was clearly a part of the Z3 family, its bodyshell incorporated some significant changes over its lesser siblings, some of which were to reflect its much higher price and some of which were necessary because of the mechanical changes. Unlike any of the other Z3 models, the M Roadster was fitted with a power-operated roof mechanism. There was an aggressive front air dam that gave the car a more brutal look than the standard car, but in typical BMW fashion it was still reasonably subtle. This wasn't just for show – the extra downforce generated by it would be essential in retaining the car's high-speed stability. The lower front panels were also modified to help the brakes keep their cool – in place of the fog lights normally fitted, the M Roadster had scoops to direct air on to the front braking system to ensure it didn't overheat. The clear indicator lenses were an established M-car trademark and the chromed vent behind the wheelarches added a touch of class to a styling cue that was already present on the car anyway. A new style of wing mirror was introduced on the M Roadster to

The M Roadster's rear suspension needed a lot of work before it was capable of coping with the available power – some say it still didn't manage it. (BMW)

further differentiate it and at the rear there was a new valance to incorporate the pair of twin exhausts. In the process the numberplate was moved from the bumper to just above it with the BMW badge also being moved up – changes that sound very small, but which were very effective in giving the car a subtly different look.

Altering just the exterior detailing would have made it very difficult to justify the large price hike of the M Roadster over the Z3, so the interior was also freshened up, to make its occupants feel a bit more special. The dashboard and door trims were swathed in leather which contrasted with the trim fitted to the rest of the car and a new design of seats was fitted, which had a different shape from normal. These seats also featured two-tone leather trim, along with electric adjustment and were much more supportive than the seats normally fitted to the Z3. Brightwork was fitted around the cabin to inject a bit of life into it – as well as the instrument bezels, the door pulls, gearshift gate and ventilation controls were all detailed with a bit of chrome. The instrument count was up as a trio of extra dials was fitted in the centre console and the M logo was dotted about the cabin, although this was kept pretty discreet. A three-spoke M wheel was fitted, which was smaller and more chunky than the standard unit and the gearknob was illuminated when the headlights were switched on – although quite why this was thought necessary is anybody's guess. At the same time, kickplates carrying the M Roadster name were fitted in the door jambs and a rather nice finishing touch was the availability of chromed roll hoops behind the front seats. They gave the car a very classy look, but unfortunately their installation meant the mesh wind blocker which cut down buffeting in the cabin could no longer be fitted.

Although some of these changes were functional rather than merely cosmetic, under the skin there were more changes that differentiated the M Roadster from the Z3. The floor pressing was completely different to allow for the exhaust layout that was unique to the car. Because the M Roadster was fitted with a pair of silencers, the battery could no longer be positioned on one side of the boot. That meant it had to be located in the middle, which then displaced the spare wheel. But there was nowhere left to house this, unless the whole boot was going to be filled up. The only answer was to do away with it altogether, and in its place fit a small tyre compressor with a tube of sealing compound. Just in case this wasn't enough, BMW offered a service whereby a stranded owner could call a helpline and be rescued with a replacement wheel and tyre.

The US M Roadster

As soon as the M Roadster went on sale it proved to be a success – especially in the American market which snapped up the car at a rate three times greater than across the whole of Europe. It was just as well the car proved to be a success in the USA because BMW had needed to redevelop it especially for that market. Like the European car, the US M Roadster was heavily based on the home market M3, which meant that under the skin the American M Roadster was quite a different car from its European counterpart. Instead of the 3,201cc straight-six of the standard car, the US-bound M Roadster had a 3,152cc engine fitted which had already been homologated for the M3 Evo. This meant 240bhp and 236lb ft were on offer, although the torque curve was flatter than that of the European car, making it more pleasant to drive at 'normal' speeds.

To ensure that the American M Roadster was still capable of ridiculously quick acceleration, a lower final drive ratio was fitted than was standard on its European counterpart. This allowed the car to sprint from a standing start to 60mph in a claimed 5.2 seconds – which was not only plenty quick enough for most buyers of the car, but was also on a par with the more powerful M Roadster sold in Europe. The top speed was reduced to an electronically limited 137mph (220kmh), but in a country where 55mph (88kmh) was the maximum anyway, such a 'low' top speed was hardly a hindrance.

There were few other changes made to the M Roadster for it to be sold in the USA – the same interior and exterior modifications were carried out although just two extra gauges were fitted in the centre console instead of three and there were minor changes made to the numberplate lighting arrangements so that it would comply with federal laws. Because the car's top speed was lower, there was less sound proofing fitted, in a bid to make the car a little less refined and a little bit more raw – but it wasn't really enough because the American motoring press still felt something was missing. While the scorching acceleration was something that could be exploited to the full most of the time thanks to the capable chassis, it wasn't as involving to drive as it should have been, because it was still too refined.

Z3 facelift

With such long model cycles, BMW tends to facelift its cars every few years to keep them reasonably fresh – although with demand often exceeding supply, it probably makes little difference in terms of maintaining

The revised Z3 of 1999 didn't look much different on the outside – most of the changes were under the skin. (BMW)

At the same time as the revised Z3 being introduced, a speedster-style cover also became available. Few bought it. (BMW)

A year after the 1.8 and 1.9-litre cars were fitted with 2.0-litre engines, the 2.8-litre car was fitted with the 3.0-litre unit as seen in the rest of the 3-Series range. (BMW)

the cars' popularity. The Z3's facelift came in 1999, when the old 1.8-litre and 1.9-litre engines were replaced by new 1.8-litre and 2.0-litre powerplants respectively. Although the new 1.8-litre unit retained the same displacement as the old one (1,895cc), it was a completely different engine, and was the same as that used in the E46 318i launched in 1998. The old unit had to be replaced because it was no longer clean enough for European emissions regulations – the new one was not only cleaner than the old, but it was also significantly torquier lower down the rev range. The numbers weren't that different from the old unit, with 118bhp available compared with the 113bhp previously on offer. The peak torque figure also wasn't raised by that much, with 133lb ft generated in place of the previous 124lb ft. But despite just two valves per cylinder, the new engine was a definite improvement over the old.

The M Coupé

At a time when two-seater roadsters were becoming popular around the world, the decision by BMW to offer a closed version of its Z3 was rather an odd one.

One of the reasons for the M Coupé's popularity was its practicality. Its stiffer bodyshell also made it a better drive than the M Roadster. (BMW)

The M Coupé may have had distinctly odd proportions, but it certainly had its devotees – partly because it had no direct rivals. (BMW)

Instead of simply being a hardtop version of the roadster, the new car was to feature a more practical – if somewhat ungainly – estate-style rear end. The car came about because some of the team involved in developing the roadster felt there was scope for a closed version of the car that was a bit different. They worked on the project in their own time and came up with something that the board of BMW thought would be worth putting into production. In fact they were so sure of the car's potential that they reckoned the closed car could account for up to 20 per cent of Z3 sales, or 20,000 cars annually.

From the car's nose to the A-pillars it was the same as the standard Z3, but after that the Coupé was all new. The roof was made of steel and the rear side windows were fixed – initially the classic hockey stick C-pillar was tried, but it didn't translate very well so a more conventional straight line was chosen. The rear lights were changed so that they wrapped around the top-hinged tailgate while at the top of the hatch there was a spoiler to reduce lift and improve the car's lines. Although the Coupé would only ever appeal to a limited number of buyers, it was always rated higher as a driver's car than its open-topped brother because of its much stiffer bodyshell. An open-topped car will never have a bodyshell as stiff as a closed one, and by increasing rigidity the suspension was tweaked by Motorsport to give a car which was much more predictable on the limit.

At first, the plan was to offer the same engine line-up in the M Coupé as in the roadster, but it didn't take long for the company to realise that such a move would dilute the brand a little bit too much – instead the decision was taken to restrict availability to six-cylinder powerplants only. Even then, only the M version was offered in some markets, restricting sales of the car even further. For example, in the UK, only the M Coupé was offered, whereas in some European markets, buyers could specify the 2.8-litre engine and later the 3.0-litre unit. There were even automatic transmissions available, although the five-speed unit was too bulky to fit into the car's bodyshell, so the self-shifting gearbox had just four ratios.

Facelift

In March 2001, updated versions of the M Roadster and M Coupé were introduced. Featuring the 3.2-litre straight-six engine built for the new M3 and a five-speed gearbox, both cars developing 325bhp, up from the 321bhp of the previous models. Acceleration time from a standing start to 62mph was 5.3 seconds for both models, a reduction of 0.1 seconds, while the maximum speed remained the same at an electronically limited 155mph.

Although amendments to the cars were few and far between, there were some equipment changes. The third generation of dynamic stability control (DSC III) was fitted along with dynamic brake control. Inside, there was a new rev counter with integrated oil temperature display, already seen on the M5 and the new M3, and chrome shadow alloy wheels. Tyre defect indicators were fitted as standard and there were two

Some markets were offered 'cooking' six-cylinder versions of the Z3 Coupé, so that not all buyers had to purchase an M car. (BMW)

new colours: Phoenix Yellow and Laguna Seca Blue. Demand for the Z3 remained high – the facelift made no difference to its popularity – but more discerning drivers knew a clean-sheet design was needed to make the Z a true driver's car, and when the new car arrived, they weren't disappointed.

The Z4 arrives

Towards the end of Summer 2002 the first official pictures of the Z4 were released, and it caused quite a stir. Chris Bangle had been getting ever bolder with BMW's production designs and after the new 7-Series had been introduced the previous year – a car which certainly made you sit up and take notice – everybody was wondering how far he would go with the Z3 replacement. The 'flame-surfacing' of the X-Coupé prototype was likely to make it into production in some

The Z3 Sport Roadster arrived in 2001 and was fitted with M sport suspension, leather trim, traction control and a limited-slip differential – among many other things. (BMW)

The Z4 was much more muscular than the Z3, which had often been criticised for being too pretty and too soft – it was also much better to drive than the Z3. (BMW)

form – but what everyone wanted to know was just how watered down would it be? In the event the car was pretty radical after the Z3, but compared with the 7-Series it was really quite easy on the eye. The Z4 was certainly bold and the much more rounded nose didn't look especially aggressive, but the proportions were those of a classic roadster: a long bonnet and very little rear overhang with a short boot and not especially large cockpit. Crucially, the Z4 carried its own E number (E85), which marked it out as a model quite separate from the 3-Series – the Z3 had carried the same E36 tag as its 3-Series contemporary (despite large chunks of the E30 being in there). Despite the different tag, the Z4 still used a lot of the underpinnings of the E46.

At first, the Z4 was available only in America, where it went on sale in Autumn 2002. By Spring 2003 the car was available in European showrooms, but British buyers had to wait until June 2003 before they could get their hands on one. The range wasn't particularly

extensive, but as has always been common practice with BMW, buyers could tailor their car to suit their requirements. So, although the engine choice was restricted to 2.5-litre or 3.0-litre straight-sixes, colour and equipment options meant no two cars ever had to be the same. The larger engine delivered up to 231bhp while the smaller one offered a maximum of 192bhp. Although a six-speed manual gearbox was available in the Z4, it was reserved for buyers of the larger engine only – anyone opting for the 2.5-litre car had to make do with a ratio less.

While the Z3's reception had been lukewarm, the Z4's was much more positive – except where the styling was concerned. The Z3's looks had been thought too soft, the Z4's were now considered to be too aggressive. But after that, it was all good news, with a much better chassis, a new generation of electronic aids to keep it all together and more space in the boot and the cabin. Performance was also strong thanks to the availability of six-cylinder engines only, but in the certain knowledge that a Z4M would be on its way, those who found even the 3.0-litre car too tame would soon be able to get their power fix.

Chapter Seven

Prototypes and concepts

In Autumn 2000, BMW unveiled a pair of cars which had never been intended to be shown publicly, but which were important in the company's product development. Although they weren't touted around the various motorshows as concepts, these running prototypes began to appear in the motoring press to show just what the company was capable of. Both of them were pretty difficult on the eye, but these cars weren't built to test aesthetics – their purpose was to ascertain how far BMW could go with some of the technology it had been developing.

The first of the two was the Z18, which was a plastic-bodied two-seater roadster which had been developed in 1995. Under the skin there was a four-wheel-drive system which was ultimately developed to become the drivetrain that would be seen in the X5. The car was

powered by the 4.4-litre V8 which would also be fitted to the X5, but unlike that car with its all-steel monocoque, the Z18's composite bodyshell weighed just 1,560kg (3,440lb) – enough to guarantee scorching performance.

The second of these prototypes was the Z22, which incorporated 70 innovations and the development of which led directly to no fewer than 61 patent applications. The car was built with the aim of producing a five-seat estate which was no longer than a 3-Series yet had the wheelbase of a 7-Series and delivered the performance of a 528i auto, while still returning 47mpg. To keep weight to a minimum the bodyshell was created from carbon fibre and aluminium with the whole thing sitting on an aluminium chassis frame. By taking this route, BMW managed to cut the

The Z18 was a bizarre confection, with an ugly bodyshell fitted with a powerful V8 engine – but it was only intended to be a test mule. (BMW)

The interior of the Z18 was more palatable than the outside, as it was much less radical. (BMW)

The Z22 was another BMW testbed, and although the rear end featured some distinctly odd lines, overall its appearance wasn't too bad. (BMW)

car's weight in half, compared with a conventional steel monocoque, and it also ensured maximum flexibility in terms of which bodystyles could be offered. In a bid to reduce construction costs the Z22's bodyshell featured

The Z22's interior was much more radical than its exterior, with a squared-off steering wheel and a minimalist design. (BMW)

just 22 components requiring only six production processes to put everything together. The equivalent 3-Series was made up of 80 pieces, which consequently made it far more expensive to put together.

Powering the Z22 was a 136bhp 2.0-litre four-cylinder engine, mounted transversely in front of the rear axle. It was an all-aluminium unit and one which was constructed purely for research and development – BMW claims it never had any plans to put it into production. Mated to a continuously variable transmission, the engine was started by the driver placing their finger on a rotary switch. Using fingerprint recognition, the onboard computer determined whether or not the driver was authorised to drive the car, and if all was OK, the driver would then use the rotary switch to select the program for the transmission.

By using a steer-by-wire system it was possible to radically alter the steering lock depending on what speed the car was doing. It also allowed the foot pedal mechanism to be displaced lengthways by 61mm, which resulted in a wider range of adjustments to the seating position. This was dubbed a Mechatronic system which was a term used to describe the mechanical system which was controlled electronically, as there was no mechanical link between the steering wheel and the front wheels. At parking speeds there were just 0.8 turns between locks but by 50mph (80kmh) this had risen to 3.0 turns. Inside the Z22 there were no conventional combination instruments. Key driving information was projected on to a head-up display on the windscreen, which meant that 7.5ft in front of the driver there was a virtual image giving information on speed, warning lights, and navigational aids. In place of conventional wing mirrors there was a monitor in the middle of the facia which was linked to a TV camera showing what was behind. To enable the driver to access the most important controls as easily as possible the steering wheel was multi-functional. This allowed the driver to change gears, set the cruise control, move the foot pedals, and adjust the head-up display.

CS1

Although the CS1, first seen at the 2002 Geneva Motor Show, was never intended to be a future 3-Series, it was aimed to slot in below the 3-Series range with the new 1-Series line-up. The reason for its inclusion here is that at the time of writing the 1-Series has yet to materialise (although it has been confirmed) but it indicates what the post-E46 3-Series will look like. The flame-surfacing so beloved of Chris Bangle and his design team is much in evidence.

In common with all BMWs, the CS1 was rear-wheel drive and its motive power was provided by a 1.8-litre version of the Valvetronic engine that was so highly acclaimed in the 318i. This unit pushed out 115bhp and 129lb ft of torque and the transmission was the sequential sports gearbox (SSG) which was available on the 3-Series Coupé at the time. This allowed the driver to change gear without having to use a clutch (there were only two pedals) although there was also the option of leaving the transmission to swap ratios altogether.

As with all BMWs, the engine was mounted longitudinally to optimise the weight distribution – an engine located transversely is great for packaging, but tends to make the car nose heavy. The 18in wheels were fitted with 215/45 tyres at the front and 235/45 tyres at the back. Slowing down the car were race-spec brakes, with six-pot calipers at the front and four-pot units at the back – with just a 1.8-litre engine it would be fair to say the system was rather over-engineered!

The mechanical specification of the CS1 was pretty academic, because it is often the engine, brakes or other mechanical systems which get downgraded in the transition from concept to production model. The important thing about the CS1 was its styling, as this was what was likely to be retained, even if it was watered down in some ways. Front and rear overhangs were very short and the emphasised shoulder line running the length of the car were some of the most eye-catching features – along with the wrap-around headlamps incorporating ring-shaped side lights. At the rear there were double circular lights which also used LED technology.

Inside the CS1 things were equally forward looking. Brushed aluminium and neoprene were used to give a

The CS1 offered a lot of hints as to how the fifth-generation 3-Series might look, despite the fact that it was actually an introduction to the forthcoming 1-Series. (BMW)

The interior and facia of the CS1 were incredibly futuristic – so much so that the basic architecture of the dash is as much as could be expected to make it into production. (BMW)

thoroughly modern look while the architecture itself shared little with anything seen on any production BMW. There was a central spine running down the middle of the car and an aluminium crossbar formed the dash, with neoprene-covered dome structures rising above it. Soft, semi-transparent materials were used to give the cabin an air of space while the dash was simplified thanks to the introduction of iDrive – which would make its debut on the 7-Series later that year.

Few liked the X Coupé when it was first shown at the 2001 Detroit Auto Show – but elements of it featured in the Z4 of 2003. (BMW)

X Coupé

When it was first seen at the 2001 Detroit Auto Show, the general consensus over the X Coupé was that BMW had lost the plot. Renowned for good-looking cars which were understated and elegant, the X Coupé was anything but. The culprit was the 'flame surfacing' that was so beloved of BMW design chief Chris Bangle – he liked it, but there were few other fans. Some reckoned the car looked as though it had been in an accident, the lines were so disjointed. It didn't help that the nearside of the X Coupé was different from the offside, with a full-width door on the passenger side to help with entry and exit to the rear seats. There were several classic BMW styling cues in evidence, the most noticeable being the double-kidney grille. But whereas the usual item was fairly understated, the X Coupé's featured a startling perforated aluminium finish. The 'hockey stick' C-pillar that has long been a BMW trademark was still there – but only on the driver's side and the asymmetrical styling meant the rear end was rather less even that it first appeared. The bootlid was rear-hinged and although when opened it took the rear wing with it on the nearside, on the offside the rear wing remained in place. Such a strange arrangement meant the rear lights had to be different from each other but according to BMW: 'Mild asymmetry is more pleasant than stringent mathematical symmetry.' It is a shame that few observers agreed.

When Chris Bangle was quizzed about the radical nature of the X Coupé, he – as you would expect – was completely confident that he would be proved right: 'When there is newness, when there is change, when

there is something fundamentally at work, people talk about it. Then later, it is understood and people look back and reference the time of change to it. The fact that the X Coupé shocks and amazes is more a reflection of how fixed ideas have become about what a car can or should be.' As a designer you would also expect him to want to try concepts which were anything but predictable, but if something breaks the basic rules of aesthetics, as this concept seemed to do, only time will tell if he was being blindly optimistic.

Under the skin, the X Coupé was equally radical, because expectations would have suggested a rear-wheel-drive layout with a powerful petrol engine at the front. The reality was a four-wheel-drive system taken from the X5 and the six-cylinder diesel powerplant taken from the 330d. Lightweight aluminium bodywork meant the X Coupé was able to make the most of the 184bhp and 332lb ft of torque on offer, and BMW claimed it was theoretically capable of 125mph and a 0–60mph time of around 7.5 seconds. Although tarmac looked like the natural home for the X Coupé, it was reckoned that despite no more ground clearance than you would find on any other sporting coupé, the car was able to go off-roading without coming unstuck. But the mere fitment of traction and hill descent controls does not an off-roader make, so it is probably just as well that such a test was never performed.

Other highlights on the show car included the 20in alloy wheels, although they weren't fitted with the usual rubber band tyres that you normally find on show stars. The 255/50 rubber fitted at the front was relatively high profile for a 21st century concept, while at the rear there were 285/45 tyres. The inclusion of run-flat technology meant a spare wheel didn't need to be housed. The five-speed Steptronic transmission was something carried over from BMW's production cars, complete with steering wheel-mounted paddle shift to put some fun back into the driving experience. Helping to keep the car on the road was a rear spoiler which popped up at anything over 68mph (109kmh) and headlamps which turned with the front wheels was another innovation – although the system relied on nothing so prosaic as sensors or hydraulics. Instead, the whole set-up was controlled by GPS, which could read the road ahead before the car had even got there. BMW claimed that the X Coupé wouldn't go into production, unless enough interest was shown. That's what had happened with the Z1, but unlike the X Coupé, that was a good looking car. But the concept was to prove more prophetic than many gave it credit

Chris Bangle

Bangle was born in Ohio in 1956 and went on to study at the Pasadena Art Centre. By 1981, he had joined Opel where he went on to design the Junior concept car and the Vectra/Cavalier. His next stop, in 1985, was Fiat in Turin, where he worked on exterior design before being appointed head of design for the company. During his time with Fiat his unusual ideas began to see the light of day as the Coupé was one of his designs, along with the Barchetta. The Bravo and Brava were also attributable to Bangle alongside the Alfa Romeo 145.

Although Chris Bangle became head of BMW's design centre in 1992, it wasn't until the 7-Series of 2002 was introduced that his controversial ideas on car design came to fruition. Concepts such as the X Coupé and Z9 Gran Turismo had shown what he was capable of, and although most people didn't like what they saw, it did show what was possible with some creative thinking.

He has come in for a lot of criticism, but one thing is for sure – Chris Bangle has given BMW a bold new look for the 21st century. (BMW)

for, because when the Z4 was revealed the following year, its front end was very similar to the one seen on the X Coupé, although the similarities didn't go much further than that, thankfully.

xActivity

The latest concept from BMW is one that is destined for the showrooms. Badged the xActivity in concept form, the car shown on these pages has already become the X3. Intended as a baby brother for the incredibly popular X5, the X3 was unveiled at the 2003 Frankfurt Motor Show, and judging by the popularity of the

3-Series and increasing sales of off-roaders, a combination of the two is set to be incredibly popular. Although the xActivity concept isn't exactly the same as the X3, there are fewer differences than there normally are between a concept and its production counterpart.

Rather than just increase the ride height of the 3-Series and call it an off-roader, Chris Bangle's design team took the approach that the whole off-road 3-Series concept needed to be revisited so that it looked like an integrated design that had been built as an off-roader from the outset. But although this approach was taken, it was never envisaged that the X3 would be a true off-roader – rather it would be a vehicle which was built for on-road use in the first instance, but which wouldn't grind to a halt when the going got rough. Having said that, the production vehicle has more ground clearance than the concept, the emphasis of which was a sporty look. As Bangle put it: 'We've gone for a functional any street, any time approach that builds on the look of the X5. It wasn't just a case of taking a 3-Series Touring and adding extra mudguards and the like. We wanted to get across the idea of all-weather, all-road robustness and a sense of inner confidence, in a unique shape.'

Being a concept car, the xActivity has to pay nothing more than a token nod to practicality. Sadly the production car had to be fitted with such mundanities as B-pillars and a proper tailgate so that it lost

something of the beach buggy look. With little attention having to be paid to production costs, the xActivity's clamshell-style load bay was changed to a more conventional split tailgate for the X3. Whereas BMW's 3-Series-based estates have always been criticised for skimping on load carrying ability, the X3 aims to change that. Despite being 116mm shorter than the X5, the X3's load bay is significantly more roomy than its bigger brother's – helped by the fact that at 4,550mm in length, the X3 is 70mm longer than the standard 3-Series Touring. Just like the exterior, the interior of the xActivity shares little in common with its production counterpart. Although the basic layout is the same, neoprene and mesh upholstery is a bit radical for BMW buyers so more predictable cloth or leather are the order of the day for the showroom model.

The xActivity was pure 330iX – a four-wheel-drive-version of the 3.0-litre 3-Series Touring sold in European markets. Because the car was essentially a non-runner, it didn't really make that much difference what the underpinnings were, but the real thing has a drivetrain which is somewhat different. Although the road car is built for on-road use in the main, it still features permanent four-wheel drive with the rear wheels taking slightly more than 50 per cent of the torque. At the front there are MacPherson struts and the rear sees a development of the trapezoidal link system fitted to the 330iX. Everything has been uprated to cope with the car being taken off roading, but such abilities are compromised by the relatively low ride height. Accepting that few owners would stray from the tarmac, BMW has opted for sporty handling as much as possible.

BMW didn't try to hide the fact that the xActivity would become the X5's baby brother, the X3. The concept's lines hardly changed in the move from concept to production car. (BMW)

Chapter Eight

3-Series tuners

Although the 3-Series has always been available with relatively small engines, the focus of the range has been primarily on the larger powerplants, especially six-cylinder units. But no matter how far BMW has taken the 3-Series, there are always companies who are willing to go even further – in some cases, it would seem to be beyond the boundaries of reality! Things are probably made easier by the 3-Series being the baby of the BMW range, so bigger engines and transmissions from the likes of the 5, 7 and 8-Series have been readily available for transplant – which is why the 3-Series has been kitted out with anything from a V8 to a V12. Rear-wheel drive on all models also helps – putting a lot of power through the front wheels only is never a good idea, and converting from front to rear-wheel drive (or even to four-wheel drive) is very costly. So when it comes to tuning the 3-Series, it seems that the sky really is the limit.

The following modification suggestions have all come from Kieth Townsend, who runs Ultimate Cars, based in the south west of England. He's been racing an E36 318iS for several years, having uprated it further and further to the point where it is now effectively an M3, built for track use only. Having campaigned the car successfully, as well as having worked on customer cars performing all sorts of modifications, Kieth is well placed to recommend the best routes to take when trying to squeeze more performance out of a 3-Series, whether that means more power, improved handling, or better stopping power. All of the suggestions listed here are made on the basis of reliability – Kieth's 3-Series is reliable, and he races it. These rules can be broken, but the chances of the engine lasting any decent length of time are pretty much nil, so it is a choice between crazy levels of power and acceptable levels of durability.

Kieth's golden rule, whatever the changes that are being made, is to stick to original BMW parts where possible. By the time you've spent money buying aftermarket parts to uprate the chassis in any way, you could probably have fitted M3 parts, which Kieth reckons are generally better than anything else around. After all, if BMW has uprated the 3-Series to the limit – to produce the M3 – you don't really need to go beyond what that car can offer, even if the car is being built for track use only. And whether it's an E36 or an E46 that you're uprating, the advice is the same for virtually everything.

Engine

There's little point in trying to tune a four-cylinder engine, when straight out of the box the six-cylinder unit will offer so much more power and torque. Once

The sky is the limit when it comes to fitting bigger engines to the 3-Series. BMW's V12 engine has been shoehorned into the M3, although the car is a bit of a handful! (Hamann)

A bit more realistic is the V8 conversion, here undertaken by Hamann. But it is still more than anybody needs as the M3 is so good in standard form. (Hamann)

you have a six-cylinder car there are not that many things that are worth doing, because by the time you've spent money on modifying one of the small-capacity sixes you might as well have just spent the money on a larger capacity unit from the outset, which will probably yield more power and torque without any changes. On that basis, instead of heavily reworking a 2.2-litre straight six at huge expense, it would be cheaper – and probably more reliable – to simply buy an M3, which will already have well over 300bhp as standard. Kieth has even performed a 4.0-litre V8 transplant for one 3-Series owner, but the amount of work involved was phenomenal and unless you want something that's unlike anything else around – or at least exceptionally

There are plenty of suppliers of uprated suspension and brake parts for both the E36 and the E46 – some are better than others. (MK)

rare – the amount of time, effort and money needed to perform such an operation really isn't worth it.

Swapping the camshafts is the only thing that Kieth recommends, but even then, they tend to only come in at very high revs, making them most suited to track use. The same thing applies where aftermarket chips are concerned – by reprogramming the car's electronic control unit, you will only really see the benefit at higher revs. Finally, if you're considering turbocharging your 3-Series' engine, Kieth doesn't reckon it's a good idea. The engine bay is pretty cramped with the six-cylinder unit in there, and even if there's just a four-cylinder unit, the temperatures will get so high that the pistons will end up melting. Turbocharging may be possible, but it's a sure-fire way of compromising the reliability of the engine.

Suspension and brakes

Although Kieth advocates sticking with BMW parts where possible, there are exceptions to this rule – mainly in the suspension department. AC Schnitzer anti-roll bars are the best around, and it is worth fitting uprated units at the front as well as at the rear. The suspension might be tired anyway, but assuming it isn't, it is more important to have really good anti-roll bars than top-notch springs and dampers. That's because the springs and dampers fitted as standard are pretty good, while there is plenty of room for improvement where the anti-roll bars are concerned. For track use Leda suspension is the way to go, but if you're only going to be using your car on the road you would be better off looking at Eibach or Bilstein parts, which are more suited to road driving.

For the performance on offer – assuming the car hasn't been modified engine-wise – the four-cylinder cars have brakes which are up to the job. When it comes to six-cylinder cars, the best route to take is to fit an M3 system. Not only will this go straight on, but it is up to the job of hauling the car down from high speeds without suffering from fade. Pagid pads give the best performance and whether your car packs four cylinders or six, it's worth fitting them. If you're driving the car really hard – and this applies really for track use only – it is a good idea to fit 5-Series pads at the rear in place of the standard 3-Series items. This gives better braking balance as it evens out the temperatures of the front and rear braking systems.

Transmission, wheels and tyres

It is worth fitting a limited-slip differential, although if you take this route you will also need to fit a new

Fitting the correct wheels is essential – there are hundreds of designs available for both E36 and E46. (MS Design)

propshaft, which is shorter than the original. Most cars built to Sport specification will have a limited-slip diff anyway, and of course, if your starting point is an M3 you will already have one. It is also possible to fit different rear axle ratios depending on whether you want ludicrously quick acceleration or more even performance and a higher top speed. Kieth recommends keeping the ratio the same as when the car left the factory, but if you do want to change to

something else, at least you won't have to have the instrumentation recalibrated because the information is taken from a sensor on the diff itself, rather than the propshaft.

It goes without saying that when it comes to tyres you must stick to well-recognised brands to get the best levels of grip. These four points of contact are all you have to give you traction and braking, so buying some super-sticky rubber is well worthwhile. Goodyear F1s seem to give the best performance although if you're after something that has a longer life it's worth taking a look at what Uniroyal has to offer. These are quiet, durable and relatively cheap, while still offering decent levels of grip. As far as wheels are concerned, the standard BMW items are fine, but if you want something more distinctive it is easy enough to buy aftermarket units without having any problems. But bear in mind that most aftermarket units are not built to the same levels as the BMW ones, and as a result the steering will be heavier – although not unduly so.

Bodywork

The sky is the limit when it comes to fitting styling parts to the 3-Series, as there are dozens of companies producing skirts, splitters, spoilers and numerous other styling tweaks for the range. If you're after something that is more functional than stylistic, you have to remember that it is not until you are doing extremely high speeds – over 100mph typically – that any spoilers or other aerodynamic addenda will have any effect. So once again, unless your 3-Series is mainly for track use,

Alpine, the in-car entertainment specialists, built an M3 to showcase its products, but crash regulations meant it wasn't road legal. (Alpine)

There are all sorts of interior options available – anything offered by Hamann tends to be anything but easy on the eye though, as this shot of the company's E46 saloon demonstrates! (Hamann)

BMW M3 Convertible System Diagram

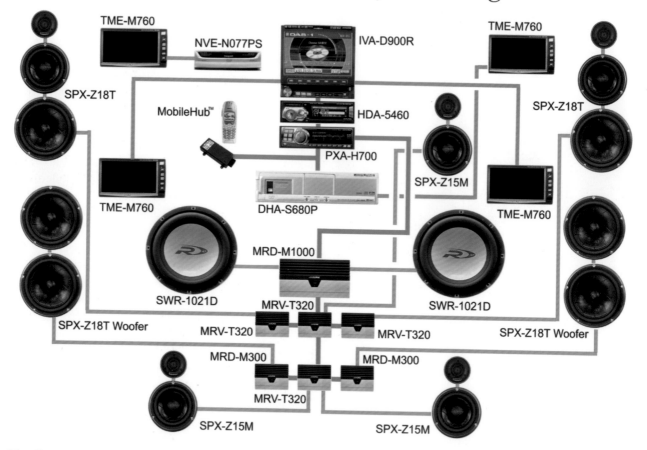

TME-M760
NVE-N077PS
IVA-D900R
TME-M760
SPX-Z18T
MobileHub™
HDA-5460
SPX-Z18T
PXA-H700
SPX-Z15M
TME-M760
DHA-S680P
TME-M760
MRD-M1000
SWR-1021D
SWR-1021D
SPX-Z18T Woofer
MRV-T320
MRV-T320
MRV-T320
SPX-Z18T Woofer
MRD-M300
MRD-M300
MRV-T320
SPX-Z15M
SPX-Z15M

When it comes to stereo installations, Alpine fitted this lot into an M3 Convertible. But the car couldn't be driven afterwards because of crash safety regulations . . . (Alpine)

Fitting jewel-style rear light clusters is popular – and for a relatively small outlay can transform the appearance of the car. This is an E36 325i. (Author)

you're unlikely to see the benefits of spending money on aerodynamic aids. But if you just want your 3-Series to stand out from the crowd, there are plenty of companies producing parts to make it more distinctive. Some of them are listed below, and although some of these companies will only do full-on in-house conversions, many of them will supply individual parts so that you can do a bit at a time.

BMW 3-Series tuners

AC Schnitzer

Apart from Alpina, AC Schnitzer is probably one of the most well-known tuners of BMWs, mainly on account of the company being established way back in 1936. Josef Schnitzer set up a garage and driving school in Freilassing near Salzburg in Austria. The business flourished, and by the time Schnitzer died in 1945, a filling station and Ford agency had been added. The business passed to the later husband of Josef's widow, Karl Lamm and in turn to Schnitzer's children – Josef and Herbert – who took it on. By 1962, the Schnitzer brothers were interested in motorsport and by 1966

Josef was driving a BMW competitively. The opening of a BMW dealership in the same year meant Josef's focus had to be on the business and the racing stopped for a while. Once the business had taken off, Schnitzer set up a motorsport division to run cars in the German Racing Car and European Touring Car championships.

Although Josef was killed in a road accident in 1978, his brother Herbert carried on running the company, and in 1982, he set up the road car tuning division. Within five years a deal was done with Kohl Automotive and that made Schnitzer a global brand as the cars were then distributed around the world. From the outset, Schnitzer's cars were anything but understated and by the time the E36 M3 was available, the company was pulling out all the stops to outdo rival tuners in the extrovert stakes.

Nearly cashing in on the hallowed CSL name, AC Schnitzer introduced its own monstrously fast coupé in the shape of the E36 M3-based CLS. Whereas many tuners lose the understated looks of BMW's cars, AC Schnitzer tends to keep things fairly discreet – or at least the customer has an option to play things down. The CLS was a case in point, as it packed a 320bhp punch yet looked only a little bit more menacing than

AC Schnitzer was one of many aftermarket tuning companies which was able to offer an uprated Z3. There were mechanical and cosmetic changes available. (AC Schnitzer)

the car on which it was based. Bulging wheelarches with 18in wheels all round suggested there was something a bit special under the bonnet and to give the interior a true race car feel there was plenty of attention paid to the cabin. The standard seats were ditched in favour of serious buckets items and carbon-fibre trim was plastered all over the place to make it look as though the car had lost weight – not that it had of course. The daft thing about the CLS was that when pitched against the standard M3, it wasn't any faster in the real world. Its top speed may have been a claimed 174mph (280kmh) against the M3's limited 155mph (250kmh), but in terms of acceleration it managed to shave just half a second off the M3's 0–100mph time of 13.0 seconds. Yet despite this, the CLS cost £71,000 – or nearly double the M3's £37,000.

Building on the idea of the CLS, there was also a CLS 2 which was based on the M3 Evolution. By upping the power to 350bhp the top speed was increased to an even more pointless 179mph (288kmh) (at least it was pointless for anybody outside Germany) and the 0–60mph time was cut down to 5.1 seconds – although once again, this wasn't that much faster than the standard car. With uprated brakes and suspension the CLS 2 cost even more than its predecessor, although at least for those who wanted to shout about their wealth, the car was rather more ostentatious than the first edition.

AC Schnitzer's CLS 2 was one of the wilder versions of the E36 M3 that was available. The interior was just as harsh on the eye! (AC Schnitzer)

For those who didn't want to buy a car as over the top as the CLS, AC Schnitzer also offered more affordable and less wild packages for most of the E36 3-Series variants. Alongside interior and bodywork modifications there were engine and suspension/braking packages to go with monster wheel upgrades. An example of something a bit more tame to come out of the AC Schnitzer factory was its 323i Coupé, which featured subtle styling changes along with some useful engine modifications to liberate an extra 12 horses. Although there were 9 x 18in wheels for those who weren't shrinking violets, like all AC Schnitzer conversions, owners could mix and match to upgrade their car however they wanted.

By the time the E46 was in the showrooms, Schnitzer had toned things down a little. Although flash versions of its tuned cars were still available, many customers preferred to be more discreet and in a reversal of roles, Schnitzer found its cars looking more understated than the cars rolling out of BMW M's factory. Taking the 330i-based Schnitzer C30 as an example, this supercharged version of the 3.0-litre 3-Series was a genuine alternative to the M3, although unlike the standard M offering, the Schnitzer could be ordered in Touring form. With 295bhp on tap, a top speed of 165mph (265kmh) and a 0–62mph time of 5.6 seconds meant the car was snapping at the heels of BMW's most rapid factory 3-Series and if the car was ordered without the garish graphics and eye-catching 19in

wheels the C30 could rightfully claim to be one of the ultimate Q-cars.

AC Schnitzer
KOHL Automobile GmbH
Neuenhofstraße 160
52078 Aachen
www.acschnitzer.com

Alpina

Probably the company most regularly associated with tuned BMWs is Alpina, the automotive tuning division of which was founded in 1965 by Burkard Bovensiepen in Buchloe – just 60 miles from BMW's headquarters in Munich. Alpina had originally been set up by Rudolph Bovensiepen to produce office machinery. His son Burkard bought a BMW 1500 and with just 65bhp on tap he found it rather lacking in the performance stakes. His answer was to devise a twin-Weber conversion to make the car somewhat more urgent.

Although at first the company worked on cars other than BMWs, it soon gained a reputation for specialising in cars made by the Munich-based company. Once a close working relationship had been established with BMW, Alpina didn't need to look back and by the early 1970s some stunning cars were coming out of the Alpina workshops. Although Alpina is still independent, it works so closely with BMW that many think of it as being a subsidiary. But the company doesn't like to think of itself as a converter of somebody else's cars – instead it prefers to see itself as a manufacturer of bespoke vehicles, and since 1983 it has been registered in its home country as such. But for the sake of

Alpina is probably the best-known of all the BMW tuners, although the company sees itself as a manufacturer rather than a tuner. (Alpina)

simplicity, in this book I'm considering Alpina to be a tuner – after all, its cars are so closely based on those of BMW's, that this is not unreasonable.

Unlike many of the younger tuning companies which have worked on the 3-Series, Alpina has modified all four generations of the car. The E21 and E30 were successful for Alpina and by the time the E36 was introduced, the sidestripes and spoked alloy wheels seen on those earlier cars had become Alpina trademarks. UK buyers didn't take to the stripes running down the entire length of the body and as a result many of the UK-supplied cars didn't feature them, but the aggressive front air dams and hoop rear spoilers were par for the Alpina course.

The first of the Alpina E36-based cars was the B6, which was launched in 1991, and was fitted with the same engine as in the last of the Alpina-converted E30s – a 2.8-litre straight-six. Developing 240bhp and 213lb ft of torque, the engine was enough to take the car to 156mph (252kmh) (with an electronic limiter) while it could despatch the 0–60mph sprint in just over six seconds. Those first cars were based on the 325i, but by 1993 the M3 had made an appearance and Alpina's B3 was starting to look distinctly overpriced. It cost DM17,000 more than BMW's M car so the answer was to introduce something that could give the new M3 a run for its money.

The 2.8-litre engine was replaced by a 3-litre unit developed from the M3's powerplant and the standard specification included leather trim, 17in spoked alloy wheels and Bilstein gas dampers. That 3.0-litre car was tagged the B3, but in 1996 the B3 3.2 arrived, which

was designed to compete with the M3 Evo launched in 1995. As with the earlier B3, there were Mahle lightweight pistons, a reprogrammed engine management system, a new exhaust system and a modified combustion chamber. The gearbox was a Getrag six-speed manual unit but there was also the option of a Switch-Tronic semi-automatic transmission. To improve braking and handling, Alpina installed Bilstein shock absorbers, Eibach springs, uprated anti-roll bars front and rear, a new stabiliser, and larger brake discs with floating calipers. Exterior changes included a new front spoiler, Alpina wheels, an optional rear spoiler and optional Alpina decals.

Alpina also reworks interiors, with plenty of hand-stitched leather and Alcantara. The basic cabin architecture isn't altered though. (Alpina)

But these six-cylinder cars paled into insignificance in 1995 when the incredibly quick 4.6-litre V8-engined B8 was launched. With a V8 engine based on the 4.4-litre unit normally seen in the 540i, this 333bhp monster was built between 1995 and 1998. During that time 231 examples were produced, along with another four slightly detuned versions which were built for Japan. A six-speed manual gearbox was produced by Getrag and the engine blocks were specially cast by BMW for Alpina, with higher compression Mahle pistons and adjusted valve timing. As well as this, there was a new exhaust system and new catalytic converters. Exterior differences included a new front spoiler, an optional rear spoiler, optional Alpina decals and 17in Alpina wheels.

When the E46 replaced the E36, there was still a B3 in the Alpina range. But whereas the outgoing model featured a 3.2-litre engine, the new car's powerplant had grown to 3,300cc. With 292bhp and 247lb ft of torque on offer, it was certainly quick, but it was also

very expensive at £41,950 in the UK. Bearing in mind the B3 was based on the 328i, which was listed at just £28,150, it needed to be pretty special to be worth nearly 50 per cent more. But then the 328i wasn't *that* special to drive – well, not compared with a B3 anyway.

Alpina's Switch-Tronic system

Fingertip-controlled semi-automatic gearshifts were largely the preserve of Formula One drivers when Alpina introduced its Switch-Tronic system in 1994. Although Porsche had its Tiptronic gearbox and BMW its Steptronic system, the first road car transmission which could be controlled by buttons on the steering wheel was Alpina's Switch-Tronic. The set-up was developed between Alpina, Bosch and ZF and the basic unit is the ZF 5HP automatic transmission. By selecting the 'S' (for Switch-Tronic) mode, the current gear is held and by using the up and down buttons on the steering wheel the gears could be selected.

Everything is controlled electronically, so that the engine can't be over-revved by changing down too early and the next higher gear will be selected if the red-line is hit while the car is accelerating. If the car comes to a

Alpina will work on any bodystyle, whether it is saloon, Coupé, Convertible or Touring. This is the company's B3, based on the E46 330i. (Alpina)

Breyton tends to keep things fairly understated, as with this E46 saloon. Recognising that BMWs are well-engineered anyway, most of the company's efforts are spent on exterior modifications. (Breyton)

halt, second gear is automatically selected, although it is still possible to change down to first gear if necessary. If too high a gear is chosen and a sudden burst of acceleration is needed, the kickdown facility allows the car to accelerate quickly by selecting a lower ratio in double-quick time. Because of the control offered by the transmission as well as the convenience, few people chose anything other than Switch-Tronic-equipped Alpinas – as a result, the company now offers nothing else.

www.alpina.de

Breyton

It was in the mid-1980s that Edmund Breyton started selling tuned BMWs, and although those initial cars were relatively tame, by 2000 the company was producing what it claimed was the most powerful 3-Series anywhere in the world. Powered by a 528bhp engine, there would be few challengers to such a claim. But with such superlative engineering on offer straight out of the BMW factory, Breyton is one of the few tuners which doesn't feel the need to sell massively powerful engine packages. Instead, it promotes exterior changes which make the car look more muscular but doesn't necessarily shred its tyres every time the loud pedal is pressed. Having said that, buyers of Breyton-

tuned BMWs can still take the mega-power route, and there's still a 528bhp E46 available. Incredibly, this powerplant displaces just 3.2 litres, but thanks to a supercharger it will also develop 403lb ft of torque and accelerate from 0–62mph in just 4.9 seconds before topping out at 205mph (330kmh). Trying to match or beat that is probably pretty pointless . . .

BD Breyton Design gmbh
Giessereistrasse 14
d-78333 Stockach
Germany
www.breyton.de

Hamann Motorsport

Hamann started out in 1986, focusing solely on the customising of BMWs. The first car was a turbocharged E30 M3 with a 348bhp powerplant that would take it from 0–62mph in just 5.1 seconds. By the time the E46 had been around a couple of years, Hamann had managed to get steadily more crazy with its conversions to the point where the Laguna Seca II made it debut to celebrate the company's 15th birthday.

Some of the wildest BMW-based creations come out of Hamann's work-shops. This is the ludicrously overstyled E46 Las Vegas Wings. (Hamann)

With gull-wing doors and a 480bhp 6.1-litre V12 engine, the new arrival was capable of 195mph (314kmh) – and cost DM500,000. As its name suggested, there had been a first Laguna Seca, which was based on the E30 M3 – and which was the first car built by Hamann which could crack 300kph (187mph). Based on an E46 M3 bodyshell, the major talking point of the Laguna Seca II was the doors, which swung upwards on an outboard stainless steel hinge fixed above the door mirrors. Other exterior modifications included a front splitter, headlight covers, a roof spoiler and a competition rear wing.

Topping the Laguna Seca II was never going to be easy, but Hamann managed to pull it off with the launch of the Las Vegas Wings at the 2002 Essen Motor

Show. Powered by a 485bhp V8 engine (based on the M5's unit), the new car cost 'just' DM280,000, yet was slightly quicker than the Laguna Seca II which preceded it – and which cost nearly twice as much. Once again the car was based on the M3 and to make it even more outrageous than the Laguna Seca II, it was finished with liquid silver metallic paint to give a mother-of-pearl effect. Topping that will prove rather difficult!

Hamann Motorsport
Im Eppen 24
D-89185 Hüttisheim
Germany
www.hamann-motorsport.de

Hartge

Whereas many BMW tuners try to lose the understated looks of the standard cars, Hartge is one of those which ensures they are retained – the term Q-car was

invented for the output of this German tuning company which, like Alpina, is legally classified as a car manufacturer in its home country. The H50 is a case in point, as it was an E46 3-Series (using whichever bodystyle you wanted) but with the mechanicals of an E39 M5, which meant that although it looked almost as innocuous as a 318i, the H50 actually had a 400bhp 369lb ft V8 sitting under the bonnet. The most significant external changes were the adoption of 19in wheels, shod with 235/35 rubber at the front and 265/30 at the back – menacing and just enough to lift the tone without giving the game away. Thanks to less weight than an M5, it was also faster and because it had more power than an M3, it was also faster than that as well. Because of the great attention to detail paid to the suspension, the 186mph top speed and 0–60mph time of 4.7 seconds could actually be used without fear of the car taking off. Brakes were also seriously uprated,

Hartge has done some madly over-the-top cars, but it has also created some beautifully understated powerhouses as well. (Hartge)

but they still fell short of the M3's system. Naturally, the ventilated discs were cross-drilled but they were 'just' 315mm at the front and 312mm at the rear. At £70,000, the H50 was hardly a bargain – especially when you consider that it might be faster at the top end than an E46 M3, but its sprinting ability was not fast enough over the standard car, even if 0–100mph in 10.1 seconds was indecently quick. This is why most buyers were happy to purchase the M3, which cost little more than half as much.

Herbert Hartge GmbH & Co. KG
An der B 51
66701 Beckingen
Germany
www.hartge.de

Racing Dynamics

Perhaps the maddest ever tuned 3-Series was an E36 Compact produced by Racing Dynamics in 1997 and dubbed the K55. Bearing in mind the Compact was the smallest car in the BMW stable, whoever decided that fitting a V12 engine from the 850CSi was clearly exploring the boundaries of sanity. In fact, they may have breached those boundaries, because instead of just taking the 850's powerplant and installing it in the Compact, the bore was increased by 7.5mm to raise the displacement from 4,988cc to 5,486cc. As well as oversized valves and new pistons, a more free-breathing exhaust system was installed and the fuel injection was remapped. All this was enough to increase the power output to 427bhp at 5,900rpm and the peak torque figure was 405lb ft at 4,100rpm. The 850 CSi's six-speed manual gearbox was also fitted and because there was no way the standard Compact's rear suspension would be up to the job, the M3's superb Z-axle was installed instead.

Of course, the wheels, brakes and tyres were also upgraded massively, but despite the latter being 8.5in wide, there was still no hope of controlling the enormous power available. For your £70,000, the K55 delivered 190mph (306kmh) performance and unbelievably, when one journalist drove it, he claimed that stability was good all the way up to 180mph (290kmh) – it is amazing what an upgraded front air dam and rear spoiler can achieve.

Racing Dynamics S.p.A
Via dei Cracchi, 20
I-20146 Milano
Italy
www.racdyn.com

And some of the rest . . .

There are dozens of companies producing their own upgraded and uprated versions of the 3-Series. Some offer outrageous conversions to everything – engine, transmission, suspension, bodywork and interior – while others will merely make the car more outspoken without changing anything under the skin. It would have been easy to have given all the pages in this book over to companies which tune BMWs, so for the sake of brevity, here are brief details of those who can help you in your quest for a more individual E36 or E46.

Evolution 2
PO Box 137
Tadworth, Surrey, England KT20 6PL
www.evolution2.co.uk

H&H Motorsport
www.hundh-motorsport.de

Iding Power
www.idingpower.co.jp

Kelleners
Am Pfauenzehnt 23
D - 46539 Dinslaken
Germany
www.kelleners-sport.com

Kerscher Tuning GmbH
Eggenfeldener Str. 46a
84326 Falkenberg
www.kerscher.de
www.kerscher-tuning.de

Lorenz GmbH & Co KG
Fritz Reuter Str. 1-5
D-49525 Lengerich
www.lorenz-tuning.de

MK Motorsport
Krankenberg GmbH
Industriestraße 20
76470 Ötigheim
Postfach 45
76468 Ötigheim
Germany
www.mk-motorsport.de

Mosselman Turbo Systems BV
Achterdijk 2
4241 TG Arkel
Holland
www.mosselmanturbo.com

MS Design
MS Design Auto-Tuning GmbH
MS-Design-Strasse 1
A-6426 Roppen
Austria
www.ms-design.com

MVR - Martin Veyhle Racing
Berliner Straße 55
71229 Leonberg
Germany
www.mvr-racing.de

RD Sport (the US division of Racing Dynamics)
11397 Slater Avenue
Fountain Valley, CA 92708, USA
www.rdsport.com

Rieger Tuning Kfz-Kunststoffteile und
    Tuning GmbH
Am Rieger-Tuning-Ring
Weilbergstrasse 16
D-84307 Eggenfelden, Germany
www.rieger-tuning.net

Torque Developments
33 Trafalgar Business Park
River Road, Barking
Essex, England, IG11 0JU
www.tdi-plc.com

Ultimate Cars
Unit 2, Quarry Bridge Works,
Chester Lane,
Cirencester, Gloucestershire
England GL7 1YD
01285 655 755

van Aaken Developments Ltd
Telford Avenue
Crowthorne, Berkshire
England, RG45 6XA
www.vanaaken.com

MS Design tends to produce discreet versions of the 3-Series and E36 Compact as here, which look sporty without being too flash. (MS Design)

Welsch Tuning
Mainzer-Str. 29
63897 Miltenberg
Germany
www.welsch-spezial.de

Wiesmann GmbH
Vertragshändler der BMW AG
Dammweg 1 (B51)
D-48249 Dülmen
Germany
www.wiesmann.de

Zeemax
The Old Thatch
Caston Road
Griston
Norfolk
England, IP25 6QD
www.zeemax.com

Zender
Auf dem Hahnenberg
D-56218 Mülheim-Kärlich
Germany
www.zender.de

Chapter Nine

The 3-Series in motorsport

This isn't intended to be an exhaustive review of the many successes of the 3-Series in motorsport around the world. Instead, this is a summary of some of the car's achievements over more than a decade of racing – factory-supported competition successes, as well as those achieved by privateers.

By the time the E36 was in production, it was accepted that the car would be entered into motorsport

around the world. BMW had started to take part in Touring Car racing back in the 1960s, initially with four-cylinder saloons then later on with increasingly specialised six-cylinder coupés. Both the E21 and the E30 had been entered in various race series so it would have been inconceivable for the E36 and E46 not to be.

318i

The first time an E36 was seen on the race track was in 1992, when BMW focused on Group N races. In Germany, the factory entered 325i Coupés but because

BMW Motorsport was started in the 1970s, producing such icons as the 3.0 CSL 'Batmobile', seen here racing at Spa Francorchamps. (BMW)

Paul Rosche is the man behind the huge success of the M brand – the BMW division largely responsible for the company's motorsport success. (BMW)

The E21 3-Series was also entered into the German Touring Car Championship. This view from 1977 shows the car of Manfred Winkelhock, Marc Surer and Eddie Cheever. (BMW)

British Touring Car racing rules precluded anything larger than 2.0 litres, it was race versions of the 318iS which were used instead. The two-door bodyshell was generally (but not exclusively) favoured over the four-door for weight reasons and that first season went very well for BMW, with Tim Harvey winning the 1992 British Touring Car Championship in a car prepared by Vic Lee. The following year was just as successful, with Roberto Ravaglia winning the Italian Touring Car Championship, while Jo Winkelhock secured victory in the British equivalent, in a car prepared by AC Schnitzer.

For 1993, the FIA introduced a Super Touring 2-litre category, and as a result, the 318i became BMW's championship contender. This was the year in which the E30 M3 had gone out of production and the E36 was still on its way, having made its official debut at the end of the previous year, therefore few international races featured an M3 on the grid. But the M-powered cars didn't disappear altogether as the M3 GTR made its debut in the newly introduced Warsteiner-ADAC-GT-Cup series. The cars were piloted by Kris Nissen and Johnny Cecotto and with 325bhp on tap and a kerb weight of just 1,300kg (2,867lb) the cars were hugely competitive. The result was a series win for Cecotto.

In a bid to increase power even further, the car became the 318iS in 1994, with four-valve heads. They

Above: The 318i, and later the 318iS, were key to BMW's international circuit racing strategy. This is the 318iS, seen competing at Spa Francorchamps. (BMW)

Below: During the 1990s, Johnny Cecotto was one of BMW's star drivers – here he is at the wheel of a 320iS, competing in the SuperTouring Car Cup. (BMW)

were prepared by AC Schnitzer for BMW and they were just as successful as the earlier cars, with Cecotto once more taking victory in the 1994 German Touring Car Championship. It was an evolution of the 318iS which led to a spin-off road car called the 318iS Class 2, sold only in Germany and which featured a rather obvious body kit that was hardly typical BMW. Unlike the racers, the road car didn't feature a six-speed sequential manual gearbox.

The four-door bodyshell had superseded the two-door by 1995, and in that year the 318i that was campaigned by Johnny Cecotto and David Brabham clinched the British Touring Car Championship. The cars were equipped with 1,998cc four-cylinder engines with four-valve heads which could develop 285bhp and 184lb ft of torque. But victory wasn't restricted to Britain – Yvan Muller won the French Supertourisme series and Jo Winkelhock won the German Super Touring Championship. In 1996 Audi took pole position in the German Touring Car Championship but for BMW the news was better the following year, when Paul Morris won the Australian Super Touring Championship.

Throughout the 1990s the rules had evolved so that BMW's Coupé-based racers became decreasingly competitive – regulations were changed so that cars with front-wheel drive were granted a 50kg (110lb) minimum weight advantage. By 2000 BMW had decided to withdraw from international Touring Car racing, concentrating its motorsport efforts (and budgets) instead on Formula One.

BMW's diesel racer

BMW didn't abandon motorsport (other than F1) altogether, and by 1998 the company was ready to demonstrate its commitment to diesel engines. Oil-burning powerplants were becoming increasingly common across Europe although America was still uninterested thanks to low petrol costs that made frugality less important than high levels of refinement. Although the six-cylinder 325tds might have been the obvious choice, purely on account of its configuration and capacity, it was actually the 320d which formed the basis for BMW's first diesel assault on the Nürburgring 24 Hours in June 1998 – which the car won outright.

The 320d was the first diesel-engined car entered by the factory in international racing – and it was extremely successful. (BMW)

Driving the first of the race-spec 320ds were Hans-Joachim Stuck, Steve Soper and Didier de Radiguès. In the second team, Christian Menzel, Marc Duez and Andreas Bovensiepen lined up to do battle. They were able to take advantage of the increased frugality of the diesel engine to the extent that the number of fuel stops they had to perform was halved and the added bonus of the oil-burning engine was its high level of torque – with 295lb ft available it didn't matter so much that the red line was set at 5,000rpm. There was also more than 200bhp on offer from the heavily revised turbocharged 1,950cc engine – a useful increase over the standard car's 136bhp.

Although BMW chose not to take the same route with the E46 3-Series, once the new model had been released, the Italian MAXteam raced one successfully in endurance racing. The car was a 320d which was raced without factory backing, although the team was given permission by BMW Italia to paint the car in works Super Touring colours. At the time of writing, petrol is still the fuel of choice for factory and privately backed racers, but as oil-burning engines evolve, that may well change significantly.

E36 M3

Because the E46 M3 did not arrive until two years after the 'cooking' versions of the E46 had gone on sale, the second-generation M3 had continued to be campaigned in motorsport well after it had disappeared from the showrooms. It was still winning races in 2000, with Jason Richards winning the championship in New Zealand with a DTC-spec edition. The following year, in Italy, where the Touring Car Championship was based on Group N regulations for production cars, Allessandro Bertei won the N1 category in his E36 M3. But it wasn't only the E36 M3 that was being campaigned – the 325i was also a popular choice for privateers. Italy's Paolo La Neve won the N2 category of his native Touring Car Championship at the helm of an E36 325i while Stefano Vallie contested – and won – the N3 class in his 320i. And it wasn't just circuit racing in which the BMW could deliver – set up correctly it could also be competitive in sprinting. Although it wasn't a common choice for such racing, Xavier Riera Vilarrasa showed what could be achieved by winning the 2000 Spanish hillclimb championship with his 320i.

E46 320i

In 2000, BMW launched the 320i DTC (for *Deutsche Tourenwagen Challenge*, or German Touring Car Challenge), which was an off-the-shelf racer for teams who wanted to enter a factory-prepared car in international races such as the DTM German Touring Car series. In the car's first season of availability it won just three races, all at the hands of Thomas Winkelhock, driving for the Brinkmann team, but by the end of the year it had also managed another three placings in the DTC top ten. As well as this success in the German Touring Car series, Duncan Huismann won the 2000 Dutch Touring Car Championship behind the wheel of a 320i DTC and Arto Salmenautio finished second in the Finnish Championship.

Meanwhile, BMW was making great inroads in the European Super Production Championship which was introduced in 2001. This series was for cars which were more closely based on production cars than many of the series in which BMW had campaigned. Despite this, the cars were still closely related to the 320i DTC cars which were available in kit form to those who wanted to campaign them. Featuring the 240bhp straight-six, the car went on to win the European Touring Car Championship. It was Dutch driver Peter Kox who won the title although in total there were six nationalities of BMW dealer which funded the campaign, hailing from Germany, Holland, Belgium, Britain, Italy and Sweden.

The car was not quite so successful during the following season, although BMW did go on to take second place in the Manufacturers' Championship while Jörg Müller secured second place in the championship to emerge as BMW's top driver. Once again the cars were fielded by six national teams, but this time they were from Belgium, Germany, Spain, Britain, Holland and Sicily. The engines were slightly more powerful as they now developed over 250bhp but the might of Alfa Romeo with its 156 meant first place was always going to be quite an achievement. It took until the fifth race (at Anderstorp) for BMW to win a race, but there were other podium finishes during the season.

M3 GTR

The most powerful 3-Series ever made by BMW, the 450bhp V8-engined M3 GTR, took the ALMS (American Le Mans Series) by storm during its first season. The car made its debut on 17 March 2001, at the 12-hour race at Sebring in Florida and it went on to dominate the whole series. Four cars were entered throughout the season – two by Team BMW Motorsport and another two by American Team BMW PTG. Although the GTR didn't win its first race, it did achieve a podium finish as it came in third. The car was driven by JJ Lehto and Jörg Müller, and when the same pair raced at Jarama later that summer, they contributed to a one/two victory for Team

As soon as BMW had developed the E46 M3 GTR properly, it beat all comers. It dominated the 2001 American Le Mans Series. (BMW)

BMW Motorsport. But they didn't get pole position – instead, they came in second behind Dirk Müller and Fredrik Ekblom to take the double-win. As if this wasn't enough, the M3 GTR managed to do even better when, for the first time, both Team BMW Motorsport and BMW Team PTG entered a pair of cars each at Sears Point, later in 2001. Nothing else on the grid could compete and it was no surprise to see the cars coming home first across the line, one after another.

Although the M3 GTR had ruffled a few feathers by the end of the 2001 season, it hadn't been all that reliable when it was first introduced – although it didn't take long for it to become competitive. Considering the car was given the go ahead just six months before it made its debut, perhaps this was only to be expected – engineering, testing, then re-engineering a race car can easily take years of evolution. Having started to win races, it seemed there was no stopping the M3 GTR, and with four double victories in succession there was no way anyone other than BMW could win the 2001 American Le Mans Series.

The M3 GTR was supposed to have spawned a road car, according to the ALMS regulations, but having won the series, no road cars were ever sold. (BMW)

Chapter **Ten**

Ownership and maintenance

This chapter looks at what you need to be aware of if you're going to buy a 3-Series, and while the second part of the chapter will focus on points specific to the E36 and E46 BMWs, in the meantime it is worth mentioning the checks that you should make for any car you are thinking of buying:

Make sure the paintwork is damage-free and all the panels line up – if this isn't the case, it'll cost a packet to put right. (Author)

Exterior:

- Don't buy in the rain – paintwork maladies will be disguised
- Look at the car in natural light – street lights do a good job of masking faults
- Look along each side for ripples and uneven surfaces on doors and wings
- Check for colour differences between panels
- Peel back the sealing rubbers around the front and

rear screens and side windows, badges and door handles for a build-up of overspray

- Paint that's got a distinct orange peel finish isn't what BMW applied at the factory – find out why it's there, or even better, don't waste your time. Just walk away
- Poke around under the bonnet for flaking paint, twisted metal and signs of filler or black underseal
- Open the boot and look for signs of overspray, kinked metal or accident damage

Interior:

Because an interior is the most expensive part of a car to recondition, it is often the most telling. Bodywork can be resprayed, wheels repainted and bumpers and grilles replaced. But if the driver's carpet is worn through, the whole floor carpet has to be replaced, and that is not cheap. This also applies to the seats, which is why they rarely get replaced.

A useful interior trick is to pull out the driver's seat belt and let it go. If it rewinds smartly, the mechanism's not worn. If it doesn't ravel itself up, it's seen plenty of use and the mileage is likely to be on the huge side. Check too that the belt's not worn, frayed or fluffed along its edge. A sagging or worn-through driver's seat means that the car has covered mega-miles. And it is the same story with floppy window winders, loose switches and grubby sun visors.

There's a clear relationship between the condition of the interior and the actual mileage a car has covered. Don't be fooled by a glossy paintbooth-fresh exterior. Spend some time checking out the interior and you will get to know what the real mileage is.

- A shiny steering wheel or gearknob are pointers to a hard life and high mileage
- Look at the digits in the odometer. Are they level, crooked, scratched or marked? Check the screws that hold the instrument binnacle in place. Have they been taken out?
- A frayed backrest or seat squab are sure signs of a hard life
- Check the headlining above the driver's seat. If it's discoloured with grime, dirt or a halo of yellow nicotine, someone's been racking up the miles
- A worn and scuffed driver's sill area means a high mileage
- Scuffed kick-plates down by the pedals mean the car's seen plenty of action
- Scratched load areas on estates and hatches could mean rep's samples or builder's bricks
- Cheap seat covers hide a multitude of sins. Lift them up
- If the ignition, door and boot keys are all different, the car's had its locks changed and could be a stolen/recovered example

Leather trim may be durable, but if it's been ripped or scuffed at all, putting it right won't be cheap. (Author)

Don't forget to look at the load bay if you're buying a Touring – if the car has worked for a living the trim may be damaged. (Author)

Any rattles or untoward noises from the engine bay need to be checked closely before any money changes hands – the stakes are very high here! (Author)

Engine:

You can tell a lot by just listening to and looking at an engine, and you don't need to be an engineer. Simple things like ticking, knocking or clattering are bad news. If it is shaking and vibrating like a blender on idle, all is not well, and if it is weeping oil from its gaskets, big bills probably beckon.

Make sure you listen to the engine hot and cold. When it is cold, the oil won't have had a chance to circulate, so it is a good time to listen for death-rattles. Also, when the engine's hot, the oil will have thinned, so it won't be quietening things down. Terminal noises come from the bottom of the engine, while less life-threatening come from the top.

If you hear a knocking from the sump, it's the big-end or crank, which means an engine rebuild. A slapping noise from the middle of the engine means worn pistons, bores or both. Again, it is an engine-out job. A light tinkling from the very top can just be tappet adjustment, but a distinct and rhythmic ticking means your cam and/or followers are on their way out. A fit engine should be quiet on idle and on the road. If you can hear any metallic noises at all, either inside or outside the car, leave it alone.

A reconditioned engine is a strong selling point but make sure there's a bill to confirm the work has been done.

■ An engine on its last legs will have an oil pressure warning light that winks.

■ Low oil level on the dipstick is a sign of neglect and problems to come. Black and dirty oil means the thing's howling for a service.
■ If there's a white sludgy substance on the inside of the oil filler cap, the head gasket has blown.
■ Start the engine from cold. Any metallic rumbling or knocking means it is time to walk away.
■ Watching the tailpipe: clouds of oil-burning blue smoke mean the engine is 'shot'.
■ Turn the ignition on and check the oil pressure light works. If it doesn't, the bulb's either been disconnected or it's blown.

The test drive:

On a flat surface of road without camber, like a dual carriageway, gently take your hands off the wheel. If the car doesn't stay in a straight line, the front wheel tracking could be out, the tyres could be worn or the car could have had serious frontal accident damage.

If the car almost changes lane when you brake, there could be a seized brake caliper or serious brake imbalance. Get it checked. If the car is fitted with anti-lock brakes (ABS), check there's no-one behind and stamp on the pedal. The car should stop without the wheels locking up and the ABS light on the dash should illuminate. ABS problems can be expensive.

A juddering steering wheel between 50mph and 60mph could be as simple as the wheels needing to be balanced. If it continues throughout the speed range, there's something more serious like bent suspension or steering.

If you do not feel up to the job of making even the basic checks, have the car professionally inspected. This is not cheap to do, but if you buy a lemon you will pay more and have a lot more hassle in the long run.

Buying and owning a 3-Series

My thanks are due to Ray Jones of Nottingham-based HAC Services for all his help with what to look for when buying a 3-Series. Ray can be contacted at: HAC Service Centre, Freeth St., Meadow Lane Ind. Est., Nottingham NG2 3GT (Tel: 0115 986 2617).

E36

Engine
Of all the engines fitted to the 3-Series, the M42, with its chain-driven valve gear, is the most reliable. With the exception of the water pump and the cooling fan's viscous coupling failing – which are faults common to all

the engines fitted to the 3-Series – there aren't any typical problems with this powerplant. The viscous couplings tend to fail every 2–3 years, and there's little that can be done to prolong their life. Similarly, the water pumps fitted to these engines tend to wear out after 50,000 miles and although replacement is pretty straightforward, it's extra expense which you need to budget for. The units originally fitted had a plastic impeller, but replacement pumps were equipped with metal impellers instead.

As with all engines, the key to keeping the engine in rude health is regular oil changes – and if synthetic oil is used each time, the engine's life should be extended even further. By putting fresh high-quality oil into the sump every 6,000 miles, the lifespan of the powerplant will be maximised. If the oil isn't changed regularly, the oil feed pipes get blocked resulting in the hydraulic tappets being starved of oil – to get the best possible service out of the engine it is also worth using a flushing oil every time the lubricant is changed.

The M40 engine is not as reliable as the M42 unit mainly on account of its valve gear being belt-driven rather than chain-driven. Although the cam belts don't have a habit of breaking, if not changed every 36,000 there's a good chance that the engine will be terminally damaged by the belt letting go. Every time the cam belt is renewed the idler wheels around which it runs must also be checked. Their bearings wear and as a result cause the wheels to run out of true, so there's a good chance that if the cam belt is overdue for replacement, the idler wheel bearings are also likely to be on their way out.

The M43 engine is the most troublesome of all the four-cylinder engines, because of the rubber seal which is located between the cylinder head and the cylinder block, at the front of the unit. This seal fails and the alloy flange which locates it corrodes, which then allows coolant to leak on to the exhaust. As a result, the cylinder head has to be removed so that the flange can be renewed, which means replacing the head gasket at the same time. All this can happen from anywhere between 70,000 and 100,000 miles (112,600–161,000km) being racked up, and although the job is straightforward, the labour bills can be very high.

Six-cylinder engines give few problems generally, one of the reasons being that they are generally less stressed than the four-cylinder units. But there are a few things to look out for, the main one being evidence of overheating. What tends to happen is that number six cylinder (the one nearest the windscreen) runs hot because it is furthest away from the air flow around the engine. This causes a hot spot which then results in the

Six-cylinder engines are especially reliable, as they're unstressed. But if they've been thrashed they'll be in poor health. (Author)

head gasket failing, allowing the unit to run hot. This might be exacerbated by the impeller falling off the water pump, reducing the flow of coolant around the engine – the two problems aren't related necessarily, but they're both known to happen.

The only other common problem that occurs with the six-cylinder engines is that of the VANOS variable valve timing system getting very noisy. The M50 and M52 are essentially the same unit, but the later M52 powerplant has VANOS fitted whereas the earlier unit doesn't. Whichever engine is fitted, it should run smoothly and quietly – if it isn't, the chances are that the VANOS

The cooling system can give problems on any 3-Series, so check the coolant level and make sure the fan works properly. (Author)

system needs to be replaced, which is the only option if it's starting to get vocal.

Aside from potential problems with fan viscous couplings and water pumps, the diesel engines – whether four or six-cylinder – tend not to give any problems at all. They should have their oil changed every 6,000 miles (10,000km), but the newer units have extended this to 15,000 miles. Really cherished cars will have their oil changed more frequently than this though, to make life as easy as possible for their turbochargers.

In a bid to save weight over a conventional steel liner, the first M52 six-cylinder engines dating from 1995 used a Nikasil coating on the cylinder bore. This reduced friction while protecting the bore from premature wear, but unfortunately this coating wasn't immune from attack if there was a high sulphur content in the petrol being burned. As a result, BMW was forced to replace a lot of engines under warranty – the company claims no more than 600 or so units – and from the summer of 1997 the M52 engine was engineered to use a steel cylinder liner to prevent the problem from happening. Any car that was affected should now have a new engine, which would have been replaced under warranty, but if you're buying a six-cylinder 3-Series from the mid-1990s, with a capacity of 2.0, 2.5 or 2.8 litres, make sure it isn't still fitted with an engine that's fitted with Nicasil-coated bores.

Transmission

If you're looking at buying an automatic 3-Series, you have little to worry about when it comes to the transmission. Whether there's a four-speed or a five-speed unit fitted, problems with these gearboxes are so rare that unless there's obviously something amiss, the chances are that it'll just keep running.

Manual gearboxes are also very reliable and unless the car has been driven really hard, there shouldn't be any problems. If the car has been taken on any track days you will need to make sure the clutch isn't about to expire and that the diff is also in fine fettle. Even if the car is well maintained, the chances are that from 80,000 miles (130,000km) onwards it will need new bearings. The output shaft oil seals can also fail, so make sure there's no oil on the driveshafts – although if the seals have gone, replacing them isn't at all difficult.

It is not a fault as such, but the gearbox can be very notchy until it has warmed up – it can take 10 miles or more before its action is smooth enough to be enjoyable. The answer is to drain the gearbox of its oil

Gearboxes are long-lived but pricey to fix if they do go wrong. The rest of the transmission can also give problems. (Author)

and refill with a thinner synthetic lubricant. At idle the gearbox is likely to be a bit noisier (it tends to chatter) but the gearchange will be smoother.

Although the earlier incarnation of the SMG transmission wasn't very well received from a driving point of view, at least it is reliable. But with so few of these cars around, if you buy one so fitted and you subsequently have problems, you might struggle to find an independent specialist who is happy to work on the car. This means you will have to use a franchised dealer, which will push up the cost of maintenance, but will at least allow you to keep the car on the road. Rear wheel

A common transmission fault is that of the differential oil seals giving way, allowing lubricant to leak out. (Author)

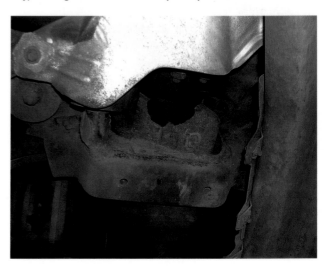

bearings don't generally last much beyond 60,000 miles (100,000km), and replacing them is quite an involved process. If you're buying a car with this sort of mileage, and the bearings are the original units, find out how much it is going to cost you to have them replaced before handing over any money.

Suspension and brakes

The fine handling of the 3-Series is largely due to a superb suspension system – which must be kept in good condition if it is to give its best. As a result of BMW's engineering, there are some parts of it which must be seen as consumables, which on other cars would be expected to last rather longer.

The first of these is the set of bushes which locates the wishbones. They perish and replacing them needs a special tool, so it is not really a job for the home DIYer. The bushes which locate the rear subframe also perish and collapse, and although it sounds like an involved process to replace them, it is actually very straightforward. The links which locate the front anti-roll bar wear out, these are also very easy to fix, as are

Any 3-Series should have fine handling. If you're looking at one that hasn't, check the rear suspension very carefully. (Author)

One of the most likely faults with the rear suspension is that of broken coil springs, although the bushes may be badly worn also. (Author)

It is not just the rear suspension that can wear out – the bushes and bearings in the front suspension also need to be checked. (Author)

Although the brakes of any 3-Series will take hard use, there is a limit. Make sure whoever is selling the car you're inspecting, hasn't breached that limit. (Author)

the front ball joints which tend to collapse. Once the ball joints start to wear the steering will pull to the left or right (depending on which wheel is affected) as the car is driven over a bump or pothole. Although replacing the ball joint is easy enough, it needs a special tool which is only likely to be held by a dealer or specialist. The final bush to check is the one located at the top of each rear shock absorber. These wear out and cause the damper to move more than it should, producing a knocking noise in the process.

The coil springs at the back of the car are prone to breaking, usually just above the bottom coil. Replacing the springs isn't easy, but if the car has been left with broken springs for a while it is probably indicative of an owner who doesn't care too much about the condition of their car. The brakes fitted to the 3-Series are very reliable, with the front discs not giving any problems. Some four-cylinder cars were fitted with drum brakes at the back and these don't give any problems. Cars fitted with disc brakes at the back – which is most examples of the 3-Series – shouldn't give any problems with the discs themselves, but it is worth taking a look at the

shoes used within the handbrake mechanism, as these can overheat, causing the brake lining to separate from the backing.

Instead of the more common metal master cylinders, BMW moved over to plastic units for the E36. Although these work fine, they can get noisy with some strange creaks appearing when the brake pedal is pressed. Spraying the pedal pivot point with silicone should quieten things down, but if it doesn't, spraying behind the rubber gaiter should do the trick.

Cars which have been driven really hard will show signs of problems with all these areas, so it is worth asking if the car has been taken on the track at all. Although this is unlikely to affect any four-cylinder cars, M3 drivers are inclined to get off the public road if they really want to open up the car – and that is when the wear rate of these components goes up exponentially.

Other areas

Whether you are buying an E36, E46, Z car or M car, you can expect perfect panel fit and ultra-slim panel gaps. Anything less means the car has received remedial work of some description at some point. Rust also isn't an issue – if the car wears the same paint and panels that it left the factory with, there won't be any rust anywhere on the car. But of course that doesn't mean you don't have to look for corrosion anywhere – inspect the car just as closely as you would any other. It's just that if you find any rust anywhere, you know the car has seen a bodyshop at some time.

A potential problem is with some of the interior fittings, which can be very expensive to put right.

If a sunroof is fitted, check that the mechanism works smoothly, that it lines up properly and that it doesn't leak at all. (Author)

Potentially one of the priciest things that goes wrong – especially if leather trim has been fitted – is the door panels breaking. The problem lies with the trim clips that hold the door in place. These break and as a result the panel gets damaged. The only solution is then to replace the whole trim panel.

The roof mechanism fitted to the convertible doesn't give problems as such, but if the car has been neglected or vandalised it'll cost a lot of money to have a new roof fitted. Although refinement levels are very good when the three-layer cloth roof is raised, there's no substitute for a hard top. These were available, painted in body colour, for all versions of the E36 and E46 Convertible, but they were also very expensive so any car that is available with one is going to demand a higher asking price than one without – but it is worth having.

Another weak spot is the window regulator, which can break. The fault isn't initially with the regulator though, as it breaks through being strained when the window itself starts to rub on the channel in which it runs. To keep everything working smoothly the channel should be lubricated at every service with silicone, but this often gets overlooked. The resulting friction then causes the regulator to get overloaded and twist before breaking.

Although there are plenty of electrics and electronics on even the most basic E36, generally they tend to be reliable. The bulb holders for the rear lights corrode and the bulbs then stop illuminating as electrical contact is lost, but a straightforward clean up will

The folding roof mechanism of the E36 and E46 are both beautifully designed – they're also very expensive to put right if damaged in any way. (BMW)

Make sure all the electronics work properly, especially costly items such as the instrumentation, climate control, stereo and security systems. (Author)

restore everything to working order. Also easy to fix, but rather more costly, is the climate control circuitry. The printed circuit board can stop working and the only way of putting things right is to replace the whole unit.

If the instrumentation stops working, there's little alternative but to replace all the dials in one go. Rather than just one instrument failing, the chances are that the whole lot will all stop working at the same time. Sometimes the gauges can read erratically if the engine is switched off then back on again fairly quickly, although things revert to normal after a few seconds. Although it might look as though the instrumentation is about to give up altogether, it is actually not a problem. A BMW dealer can reprogram the engine management system to stop it happening, but it doesn't really need it.

If the car you are thinking of buying is fitted with an electric sunroof it can suffer a few problems. The first is difficulty in closing it when really warm, because the frame heats up and moves slightly upwards. At the same time the wind deflector distorts and moves downwards, thus triggering the anti-trap mechanism. By bending the headlining down slightly it will restore everything to normal working order. The other problem that can happen is the result of voltage spikes in the car's electrical system (normally from careless use of booster chargers) which stops the roof behaving properly. By moving the roof to its tilt position and keeping the control switch pressed for at least 15 seconds the system will reset.

If the sunroof isn't opening or closing at all, it is probably because the switch has been disabled to disguise a problem of some sort. While you're checking the sunroof mechanism, also take a look at the electric windows, which can also give problems. If the switch doesn't have any effect, it is probably because the motor has failed. Although it is easy enough to put right, it's not an especially cheap job.

E46

At the time of writing, although the first E46s are already five years old, they have proved to be very reliable. While transmissions, electrics, brakes and suspension all seem to be wearing well, there are a few engine maladies relevant to the Valvetronic-equipped 318i that are worth being wary of. Six-cylinder engines are strong and long-lived and any problems that have cropped up with the 318i engine are likely to have been fixed under warranty.

Engine and transmission

The first of the four main problems which afflict the 318i Valvetronic powerplant is that of the oil pump drive coming adrift. This is held in place by a nut, but this can fall off which prevents it from being held in place. As this tends to happen when the engine is fairly new (within the first 6,000 miles is likely) any unit with a lot of miles under its belt will probably have been remedied.

Factory-fitted wheels may well need some refurbishment as they tend to get kerbed and the lacquer also weathers eventually. (Author)

If the car has been fitted with non-standard wheels, make sure there are no clearance problems by checking the inner wheelarches. (Author)

Some of the springs that make up the valve gear can prove to be unreliable, although if they do give problems it is a very straightforward job to put them right. Similarly, the thermostat for the cooling system can fail, and although this is easy enough to replace, it may seem more serious than it is. This is largely due to the car's interior heating system also failing to work, but by fixing the thermostat this should also be restored to full working order. The final problem to be aware of is one that affects the flametrap valve. This fails and consequently the engine runs erratically when air is sucked into the inlet manifold. Again, most engines will have had this repaired under warranty as the problem tends to come to light fairly early on in the car's life.

The six-cylinder cars used a plastic manifold which can crack along a seam that runs along the underside. Because this seam is out of sight it can be dificult to detect why the engine is idling unevenly, so if it is running erratically, look at the joint where the manifold sits up under the bulkhead.

Transmission faults are few and far between although the five-speed automatic gearbox has an undeserved reputation for being fragile. They are actually very tough, but it is still essential to check that it is changing ratios smoothly and there is no clutch slip because replacing such a unit is very costly. Even the four-cylinder cars are extremely smooth, so the slightest imbalance is immediately obvious. If there's any clutch judder when moving off in a manual-gearbox car it is probably because the rear gearbox mounting needs to be replaced. If the judder is really bad you will probably need to replace the engine mountings, but such cases are rare.

Brakes, steering and suspension

In common with the E36, the steering, brakes and suspension need to be kept in tip-top condition to give their best, and hard-driven cars will be suffering from wear to some components. The track control arms are the first to show signs of use, with the whole part needing to be replaced if the car has been driven at ten-tenths. If the track control arm is creaking it is because the rubber buffer in the hydraulic mount needs to be replaced, which is a straightforward job.

As with the E36 cars, the lower front ball joints wear out. The symptom of this is a vibration through the steering wheel when braking – much the same as you would get with warped brake discs. But unlike the E36, when these ball joints need replacement, the whole of

Plastic brake master cylinders can give some odd squeaking and creaking noises, but this is normal. Silicone spray normally cures it. (Author)

the alloy front arm needs to be replaced at the same time – something which can prove to be very expensive.

The brakes are up to the job on all cars, but as is the case with any vehicle, if they have been used really hard, such as on a track day, it may be that the discs have overheated and become warped as a result. If this is the case, the juddering that results will show up straight away. If you decide to replace braking components at home, make sure you're familiar with the correct procedures as the system is very complex and not that easy to work on. Cars equipped with DSC are even more complicated and to bleed the system properly the engine needs to be running.

Other potential problems

On cars fitted with early xenon lights, the headlamp washer system can leak from various places. The reservoir itself can leak gradually while the O-rings which seal the hoses to the washer pump and the jets can fail. As if that's not enough, the jet and nozzle sometimes don't clip together properly which is why the design was updated in August 1999 and then again in March 2000. Any cars after this later date will be fine – but earlier ones may not be.

Coupés suffer from an embarrassing problem whereby the door (and if you're unlucky, both doors) can't be opened from the outside. This happens because the door catch gets out of adjustment and there's not enough travel in the handle for it to do its job of unlatching the catch. The problem only affects cars with the handles which don't open upwards as they are pulled outwards, and the cure is simple enough. The door needs to be opened (from the inside if necessary) and the allen bolt in the side of the door has to be adjusted. Check how far the handle needs to travel before the rotary catch starts moving – it should be about 13mm.

Some of the early E46s used an indicator switch which is known to give problems – the switch terminals wear over time to create a permanently closed circuit so that the indicators can't be switched off. Replacing the unit with a later design of stalk will cure the problem, but bear in mind that cars equipped with an on-board computer used a different part.

A couple of electrical glitches have shown themselves to be common, although neither of them is tricky nor expensive to put right. If the airbag warning light won't go out it is probably because the wiring loom to the seatbelt pre-tensioner needs to be replaced. Although it is a quick fix, the system needs to be reset afterwards so it is not a DIY job. The other fault concerns the heater motor, which can run erratically. The cure is a new resistor pack, but before you replace it, make sure the motor is whining when run at low speed for a few minutes.

Z3, Z3M and M Coupé

Because the various engines fitted to the Z3 were all fitted to the 3-Series, the same problems and procedures apply. The two main ones are the 16-valve engines which can leak coolant down the front of the powerplant and the wearing of the Nikasil coating on six-cylinder engines. Cars built after March 1998 aren't affected by this latter problem. Transmissions are also the same as those fitted to other cars in the 3-Series range. This means automatic gearboxes are long-lived but expensive to fix when they do finally start to give problems while manual gearboxes should be fine, except for maybe a bit of recalcitrance when cold.

The rest of the mechanicals are pretty tough, although a thorough check for any untoward noises is essential. Cars built before September 1999 were prone to anti-roll bars popping off their mountings – if this has happened it will be immediately obvious, but get underneath and check that all is in order anyway.

Bodywork on any Z3 should not be an issue so any signs of rust or bodyshell flexing suggests the car has been in an accident and then poorly repaired. Scuttle shake shouldn't be there because the Z3's bodyshell is exceptionally stiff – any evidence of this means big trouble. Other than that the only likely bodywork problems lie with the front and rear bumper. With the former it is a case of the plastic mountings breaking off, while with the latter, the anti-vibration weights mounted in the bumper can start to vibrate themselves. Wrapping them in foam is the standard cure.

The most likely problem any Z3 owner is likely to encounter is the hood wearing to the point where it needs to be replaced. The problem lies in the fact that the hood fabric chafes against the hood frame and as a result some of the earliest cars have got through three or four roofs. The wear takes place when the roof is raised and lowered, so cars that have been used every day will be the ones worst affected. Replacing the roof isn't straightforward as there are all sorts of cables and flaps to keep it all tensioned, which only adds to the cost of replacement. Later cars were fitted with a three-layer roof which is even more costly to fix, but at least it makes the car much quieter than the earlier single-layer affair fitted to the first examples.

Pre-1999 cars were known for leaking roofs, the problem occurring when the seal between the roof and the bodywork perished along the back of the roof. Water would leak into the roof storage area and would then find its way into the boot, but cars built since early 1999 have been fitted with a plastic gutter to keep the area dry.

Make sure the battery tray hasn't filled up with water because the seal for the third brake light or the one for the rear lights has started to allow water in. Fixing such problems is easy because it simply means replacing the seals – less straightforward is putting right a water leak between the front of the roof and the top of the door. This involves removing the door trim and adjusting the window alignment before adjusting the tension of the locking hooks on the front of the hood.

The Z3's rear window is plastic, which means it is prone to scuffing and scratching, which will eventually render it opaque. Although there are various potions available to rub into the window and remove the scuffing, if there are any really deep scratches the window will need to be replaced. Luckily, it is not difficult to do this as it is only zipped in, meaning the roof doesn't need to be removed before the work can be done.

What the E numbers mean

Since 1963, all BMWs have been identified by an E number. There is debate as to whether this is short for entwurf (design) or entwicklung (development), but the numbers denote the order in which the designs were commenced, rather than the order of cars reaching production. Because the E numbers relate to designs rather than the cars themselves, there are many numbers unused – cars which were designed, but never made it to the production line. The E numbers BMW has created so far are:

E3	2500, 2800 and other large saloons	1968–1977
E6	Facelifted '02 cars (original 02 had no E code)	1973–1975
E9	Six-cylinder coupés (2500CS to 3.0CSL)	1968–1971
E10	2002 Turbo	1973–1975
E12	First generation of 5-Series	1972–1981
E21	**First generation of 3-Series**	**1975–1982**
E23	First generation of 7-Series	1977–1986
E24	6-Series	1976–1989
E26	M1	1978–1980
E28	Second generation of 5-Series	1972–1981
E30	**Second generation of 3-Series**	**1983–1991**
E30/5	**3-Series Touring**	**1983–1991**
E30/16	**3-Series with four-wheel drive**	**1983–1991**
E31	8-series	1989–1999
E32	Second generation of 7-Series	1986–1994
E32	Second generation of 7-Series	1986–1994
E32/2	7-Series long-wheelbase	1986–1994
E34	Third generation of 5-Series	1988–1996
E34	5-Series with four-wheel drive	1988–1996
E36	**Third generation of 3-Series**	**1991–1998**
E36/2	**3-Series Coupé**	**1992–2000**
E36/5	**3-Series Compact**	**1994–2000**
E36/5	**3-Series Touring with M52 engines**	**1995–2000**
E38	Third generation of 7-Series	1994–2001
E39	Fourth generation of 5-Series	1995–2003
E46	**Fourth generation of 3-Series**	**1997–**
E46/2	**3-Series Coupé**	**1999–**
E46/2c	**3-Series Convertible**	**2000–**

Appendix B

Engine codes

Way back in 1961, BMW started to give its engines model codes, although having started the series, the counter was reset in 1963. Since then all engines have featured an M number, although for some reason the M60 number was given to two different powerplants.

Unit	Fuel	Cylinders	Valves	Capacity	Introduction year
M10	Petrol	4	8	1.6, 1.8, 2.0	1961
M20	Petrol	6	12	2.0, 2.3, 2.5, 2.7	1985
M21	Diesel	6	12	2.4	1985
M30	Petrol	6	12	2.5, 2.8, 3.0, 3.2, 3.4, 3.5	1968
M40	Petrol	4	8	1.6, 1.8	1987
M41	Diesel	4	8	1.7	1994
M42	Petrol	4	16	1.8	1986
M43	Petrol	4	8	1.8	1993
M44	Petrol	4	16	1.8	1994
M50	Petrol	6	24	2.0, 2.5	1992
M51	Diesel	6	12	2.5	1991
M52	Petrol	6	24	2.0, 2.5, 2.8	1995
M54	Petrol	6	24	3.0	2000
M57	Diesel	6	24	3.0	1998
M60	Petrol	6			1977
M60	Petrol	8	32	3.0, 4.0	1992
M62	Petrol	8	32	3.5, 4.0, 4.4	1996
M70	Petrol	12	24	5.0	1987
M73	Petrol	12	24	5.4	1995
M88	Petrol	6	24	3.5	1979

Appendix C

Chronology

December 1990	E36 saloon introduced
October 1991	E36 325td arrived
January 1992	E36 Coupé launched
October 1992	E36 M3 coupé debuted
November 1992	E36 Cabriolet launched
April 1993	E36 325tds introduced
January 1994	E36 M3 Cabriolet launched
February 1994	E36 Compact introduced
July 1994	E36 M3 saloon debuted
October 1994	318td – new 1.7-litre diesel engine
November 1994	E38 Touring launched
February 1995	E36 323i and 328i arrived
July 1995	E36 M3 Evolution introduced
November 1995	Z3 launched in four-cylinder form
March 1996	Z3 2.8 arrived
July 1996	E36 318iS Coupé introduced
	E36 – facelift for saloon
March 1997	M Roadster debuted
July 1997	323Ti Compact launched
November 1997	E46 saloon went on sale
February 1998	E46 320d introduced
July 1988	M Coupé arrived
Autumn 1998	E46 Coupé superseded E36 models
Winter 1998/9	E36 M3 Evolution – last sold
February 1999	Z3 and M Coupé facelifted
March 1999	E46 316i launched
May 1999	E46 Touring debuted
September 1999	E46 330d went on sale
Spring 2000	330i on sale
Summer 2000	E46 Convertible on sale
Summer 2000	330d on sale
Autumn 2000	325Ci replaced 323Ci
Autumn 2000	E46 Touring arrived

Autumn 2000	E46 M3 shown
Summer 2001	E46 M3 got SMG II
Summer 2001	E46 M3 Convertible introduced
Summer 2001	E46 Compact launched
Autumn 2001	SMG transmission for 325i and 330i
October 2001	318Ti and 320td Compacts arrived
October 2001	E46 facelifted arrived
May 2002	330Ci Clubsport introduced
Spring 2003	Facelifted E46 Compact launched
Summer 2003	Z4 went on sale
Autumn 2003	330Cd launched

Appendix **D**

Specifications

To save repetition in these specification tables, it's worth mentioning that all E36 and E46 3-Series models share certain characteristics. All have fuel injection, servo-assisted brakes, power-assisted steering (except some early examples of the 316i), rear-wheel drive and monocoque construction.

E36 Specifications

316i

ENGINE:
In-line four-cylinder, alloy head, iron block, SOHC, 8 valves

Bore x stroke (mm)	84x72
Capacity	1,596
Compression ratio	9.0:1
Fuel injection	Bosch Motronic
Maximum power	98bhp@5600rpm (102bhp@5500rpm from 1993–1998)
Maximum torque	102lb ft@4250 (110lb ft @3900 from 1993–1998)

TRANSMISSION:
Five-speed manual or optional four-speed automatic
Final drive ratio	3.45:1 (4.45:1 with automatic transmission)

SUSPENSION:
Front	MacPherson struts, coil springs, telescopic dampers, anti-roll bar
Rear	Multi-link axle with central pull rod, coil springs, anti-roll bar

STEERING:
Rack and pinion
Turns lock-to-lock	5.1

BRAKES:
Front	Discs
Rear	Drums (discs from 1991)

ABS optional, then standard from November 1991

WHEELS/TYRES: 6Jx15 with 185/65 15 tyres

PERFORMANCE:
Max speed	119mph (117mph auto)
0–62mph	12.9sec (14.4sec auto)

318i

As 316i except:
ENGINE:
Bore x stroke (mm)	84x81
Capacity	1,796cc
Compression ratio	8.8:1
Maximum power	113bhp@5500rpm (117bhp@5500rpm from 1993–1998)
Maximum torque	117lb ft@4250rpm (124lb ft @3950 rpm from 1993–1998)

STEERING:
Power-assisted steering standard
Turns lock-to-lock	3.4

PERFORMANCE:
Max speed	123mph (123mph auto)
0–62mph	11.3sec (12.3sec auto)

320i

As 318i except:

ENGINE:

In-line six-cylinder, DOHC, 24 valves

Bore x stroke (mm)	80x66
Capacity	1,991cc
Compression ratio	10.5:1
Maximum power	150bhp@5900rpm
Maximum torque	140lb ft@4700rpm

TRANSMISSION:

Five-speed manual or optional five-speed automatic

Final drive ratio	3.45 (manual).
	4.45 (automatic)

BRAKES:

Rear	Discs

WHEELS/TYRES:

6.5Jx15 wheels with 205/60 15 tyres

PERFORMANCE:

Max speed	133mph (133mph auto)
0–62mph	9.8sec (10.8sec auto)

323i

As 320i except:

ENGINE:

Bore x stroke (mm)	84x75
Capacity	2,494cc
Compression ratio	10.0:1
Maximum power	170bhp@5500rpm
Maximum torque	181lb ft@3950rpm

WHEELS/TYRES:

7Jx15 wheels with 205/60 15 tyres

PERFORMANCE:

Max speed	145mph (143mph auto)
0–62mph	7.9sec (8.9sec auto)

325i

As 323i except:

ENGINE:

Maximum power	192bhp@5900rpm
Maximum torque	177lb ft@4200rpm

WHEELS/TYRES:

7Jx15 wheels with 205/60 15 tyres

PERFORMANCE:

Max speed	145mph (143mph auto)
0–62mph	7.9sec (8.9sec auto)

328i

As 325i except:

ENGINE:

Bore x stroke (mm)	84x84
Capacity	2,793cc
Compression ratio	10.2:1
Maximum power	193bhp@5500rpm
Maximum torque	206lb ft@3500rpm

STEERING:

Turns lock-to-lock	3.2

PERFORMANCE:

Max speed	145mph
0–62mph	7.5sec

M3

ENGINE:

In-line 6-cylinder, alloy head, iron block, DOHC, 24 valves

Bore x stroke (mm)	86x85.8
Capacity (cc)	2,990
Compression ratio	10.8:1
Fuel injection	Bosch Motronic 3.3
Maximum power	286bhp@7,000rpm
Maximum torque	236lb ft@3,600rpm

TRANSMISSION:

Six-speed manual

Final drive ratio	3.15:1

STEERING:

Turns lock-to-lock	2.8

BRAKES:

Front	Ventilated discs
Rear	Ventilated discs

WHEELS/TYRES:

7.5x17in alloy wheels with 235/40 ZR17 tyres

PERFORMANCE:

Max speed	155mph
0–62mph	5.4sec

M3 Evo

As M3 except:

ENGINE:

Bore x stroke (mm)	86.4x91
Capacity (cc)	3,201
Compression ratio	11.3:1
Maximum power	321bhp@7,400rpm
Maximum torque	258lb ft@3250rpm

TRANSMISSION:

Final drive ratio	3.23:1

WHEELS/TYRES:

Front:	7.5x17in alloy wheels with 225/45 ZR17 tyres
Rear:	8.5x17in alloy wheels with 245/40 ZR17 tyres

318tds

ENGINE:

In-line four, alloy head, iron block, SOHC, 8 valves

Bore x stroke (mm)	80x83
Capacity	1,665cc
Compression ratio	22.0:1
Fuel injection	Indirect
Maximum power	90bhp@4000rpm
Maximum torque	140lb ft@2000rpm

TRANSMISSION:

Gears	Five-speed manual
Final drive ratio	2.65:1

BRAKES:

Front	Solid discs
Rear	Drums

WHEELS/TYRES:

7J x 15in alloy wheel
205/60 VR15 Michelin Pilot HX tyres

PERFORMANCE:

Max speed	114mph
0–60mph	13.5 sec

325td

ENGINE:

In-line 6-cylinder, alloy head, iron block, SOHC, 12 valves

Bore x stroke	80mmx82.8mm
Capacity	2,498cc
Compression ratio	22.0:1
Maximum power	115bhp@4800rpm
Maximum torque	164lb ft@1900rpm

TRANSMISSION:

Number of gears	5-speed manual
4-speed auto optional	
Final drive ratio	2.65:1 (3.23:1 auto)

PERFORMANCE:

Max speed	123mph
0–62mph	12.0sec

325tds

As 325td except:

ENGINE:

Maximum power	143bhp@4800rpm
Maximum torque	192lb ft@2200rpm

TRANSMISSION:

Number of gears	5-speed manual
5-speed auto optional	
Final drive ratio	2.56:1 (manual and auto)

WHEELS/TYRES:

6.5x15 alloy wheels with 205/60 R15 Sport Continental tyres

PERFORMANCE:

Max speed	134mph
0–60mph	8.8sec

E46 Specifications

316i

ENGINE:

In-line 4-cylinder, alloy head, iron block, DOHC, 8 valves

Bore x stroke (mm)	83.5x85
Capacity (cc)	1,895
Compression ratio	9.7:1
Fuel injection	BMS 46
Maximum power	105bhp@5300rpm
Maximum torque	122lb ft@2500rpm

TRANSMISSION:
5-speed manual or optional 4-speed automatic
Final drive ratio   3.23:1 (4.44:1 with
                        automatic transmission)

SUSPENSION:
Front   MacPherson struts, coil
                        springs, telescopic dampers,
                        anti-roll bar
Rear   Multi-link axle with central
                        pull rod, coil springs, anti-
                        roll bar

STEERING:
Turns lock-to-lock   3.2

BRAKES:
Front   286mm ventilated discs
Rear   280mm solid discs

WHEELS/TYRES:
6.5 x 15 with 195/65 R15 tyres

PERFORMANCE:
Max speed   124mph (121mph auto)
0–62mph   12.4sec (13.6sec auto)

318i/318Ci

As 316i except:
ENGINE:
Maximum power   118bhp@5500rpm
Maximum torque   133lb ft@3900rpm

TRANSMISSION:
Final drive ratio   3.38:1

WHEELS/TYRES:
7 x 16 wheels with 205/55 R16 tyres

PERFORMANCE:
Max speed   129mph (126mph auto)
0–62mph   10.4sec (12.2sec auto)

320i

As 318i except:
ENGINE:
In-line six-cylinder, alloy head, alloy block, DOHC, 24
valves

Bore x stroke (mm)   80x72
Capacity (cc)   2,171
Compression ratio   10.8:1
Maximum power   170bhp@6250rpm
Maximum torque   156lb ft@3500rpm

TRANSMISSION:
Final drive ratio   3.38:1 (manual or auto)

BRAKES:
Rear   Ventilated discs

WHEELS/TYRES:
7 x 16 wheels with 205/55 R16 tyres

PERFORMANCE:
Max speed   140mph (139mph auto)
0–62mph   8.2sec (9.3sec auto)

323i

As 320i except:
ENGINE:
Bore x stroke (mm)   84x75
Capacity (cc)   2,494
Compression ratio   10.5:1
Maximum power   170bhp@5500rpm
Maximum torque   181lb ft@3500rpm

PERFORMANCE:
Max speed   145mph (143mph auto)
0–62mph   8.0sec (9.0sec auto)

325i

As 320i except:
ENGINE:
Bore x stroke (mm)   84x75
Capacity (cc)   2,494
Compression ratio   10.5:1
Maximum power   192bhp@6000rpm
Maximum torque   181lb ft@3500rpm

TRANSMISSION:
Final drive ratio   3.15:1 (3.23:1 with
                        automatic transmission)

PERFORMANCE:
Max speed   149mph (147mph auto)
0–62mph   7.2sec (8.3sec auto)

328i

As 325i except:

ENGINE:

Bore x stroke (mm)	84x84
Capacity (cc)	2,793
Compression ratio	10.2:1
Maximum power	193bhp@5500rpm
Maximum torque	206lb ft@3500rpm

TRANSMISSION:

Final drive ratio	2.93:1

WHEELS/TYRES:

8 x 17in with 225/45 ZR17 tyres

PERFORMANCE:

Max speed	145mph
0–62mph	7.5sec

330i

As 328i except:

ENGINE:

Bore x stroke (mm)	89.0x89.6
Capacity (cc)	2,979cc
Compression ratio	10.2:1
Fuel injection	Multi-point sequential
Maximum power	231bhp@5900rpm
Maximum torque	221lb ft@3750rpm

TRANSMISSION:

SMG transmission available from autumn 2001

Final drive ratio	2.93:1

STEERING:

Turns lock-to-lock	3.2

BRAKES:

Front	Ventilated discs
Rear	Ventilated discs

WHEELS/TYRES:

8.5x18in alloy wheels with 225/40 ZR18 tyres front and 255/35 ZR18 rear

PERFORMANCE:

Max speed	151mph (153mph auto)
0–62mph	6.7 sec (7.0sec auto)

M3

As 330i except:

ENGINE:

In-line 6-cylinder, alloy head, iron block, DOHC, 24 valves

Bore x stroke (mm)	87x91
Capacity (cc)	3,245
Compression ratio	11.5:1
Maximum power	343bhp@7900rpm
Maximum torque	269lb ft@4900rpm

TRANSMISSION:

Final drive ratio	3.62:1

STEERING:

Turns lock-to-lock	3.2

WHEELS/TYRES:

8 x 18 wheels at the front and 9 x 19 at the rear with 225/45 ZR18 and 255/40 ZR19 tyres

PERFORMANCE:

Max speed	155mph
0–60mph	4.8sec

320d

As 318i except:

ENGINE:

In-line 4-cylinder, alloy head, iron block, DOHC, 16 valves

Bore x stroke (mm)	88x84
Capacity (cc)	1,951 (1,995cc from autumn 2001)
Compression ratio	19:1
Fuel injection	Common rail
Maximum power	136bhp@4000rpm (150bhp@4000rpm from autumn 2001)
Maximum torque	206lb ft@1750rpm (243lb ft @2000rpm from autumn 2001)

TRANSMISSION:

5-speed manual or 4-speed auto

Final drive ratio	2.47:1 (2.35:1 from autumn 2001)

PERFORMANCE:

Max speed	129mph (134mph from autumn 2001)
0–62mph	9.9sec (8.9sec from autumn 2001)

330d

As 320d except:

ENGINE:

In-line six-cylinder, alloy head, iron block, DOHC, 24 valves

Bore x stroke (mm)	84x88
Capacity (cc)	2,926cc
Compression ratio	18:1
Fuel injection	DDE 4.0
Maximum power	184bhp@4000rpm
Maximum torque	288lb ft@2200rpm

TRANSMISSION:

Final drive ratio	2.28:1

STEERING:

Turns lock-to-lock	3.3

BRAKES:

Front	Ventilated discs
Rear	Ventilated discs

WHEELS/TYRES:

7x17in alloy wheels with 205/50 VR17 tyres

PERFORMANCE:

Max speed	141mph (141mph auto)
0–62mph	7.9 sec (8.2sec auto)

M Coupé

ENGINE:

In-line six-cylinder, alloy head, iron block, DOHC, 24 valves

Bore x stroke (mm)	86.4x91
Capacity (cc)	2,926cc
Compression ratio	11.3:1
Fuel injection	MS S50 DME
Maximum power	321bhp@7400rpm
Maximum torque	258lb ft@3250rpm

TRANSMISSION:

Final drive ratio	3.15:1

STEERING:

Turns lock-to-lock	3.2

BRAKES:

Front	Ventilated discs
Rear	Ventilated discs

WHEELS/TYRES:

7.5x17in alloy wheels with 225/45 ZR17 tyres front and 245/40 ZR17 rear

PERFORMANCE:

Max speed	160mph
0–60mph	4.9 seconds

Appendix **E**

Clubs

North America

BMW Car Club of America
640 South Main Street
Suite 201
Greenville
SC 29601
Tel: 864.250.0022 Fax: 864.250.0038
Web: www.bmwcca.org

BMW Car Club of British Columbia
PO Box 3452
349 W. Georgia St.
Vancouver, BC V6B 3Y4
Web: www.bmwccbc.org

BMW Car Club of Canada
203-2435 Welcher Avenue
Port Coquitlam
BC V3C 1X8, Canada
Fax: 604-945-4761
Web: www.bmwclub.ca

Asia

BMW Club of Japan
1-17-8 Numakage
Urwa Saitama
336-0027, Japan
Web: www.bmwclubs.ne.jp

BMW Car Club Malaysia
Suite B-311
Jalan SS7/26 Kelana Square
Taman Kelana Indah
Kelana Jaya, 47301
Petalang Jaya, Selangor, Malaysia
Web: www.bmwclub.com.my

Australia and New Zealand

BMW Car Club of Australia
PO Box 12491
A'Beckett Street Post Office
Melbourne
VIC 8006
Web: www.clubs.bmw.com.au

BMW Car Club of New Zealand
PO Box 7113
Wellesley Street
Auckland
New Zealand
Web: www.bmwclub.org.nz

Europe

BMW Car Club of Great Britain
PO Box 328
Melksham
Wiltshire, England SN12 6WJ
Tel: 01225 709 009
Fax: 01225 703 885
Web: www.bmwcarclubgb.co.uk

BMW Club Europa BV
Lauchstaetter Strasse 11 Geb. 8/6
D-80788 München
Germany
Tel: +49.89.382 248 20 Fax: +49.89.382 343 90
Web: www.bmw-club-europa.org

BMW Clubs Sweden
4:e Tvärgatan 60
802 82 Gävle
Tel: 026 649170 Fax: 026 649172
Web: www.bmwcs.com

Index